THE
STEM LEADER
GUIDE

SCIENCE - TECHNOLOGY - ENGINEERING - MATHEMATICS

PRACTICAL ADVICE FOR
CREATING A STEM SCHOOL

BY HANS MEEDER

ALLVIEW CREEK MEDIA

Other works by Hans Meeder

Advisory Boards That Matter
Co-authored with Brett Pawlowski

Career Pathways, Education with a Purpose
Contributor, Compiled and co-authored by Dan Hull

ALLVIEW CREEK MEDIA is a
division of the Meeder Consulting Group, LLC
6713 Groveleigh Drive, Columbia, MD 21046
Visit our Web site at www.meederconsulting.com
First Edition, July 2013

10 9 8 7 6 5 4

Meeder, Hans
THE STEM LEADER GUIDE
ISBN: 978-1-939836-00-7

Cover design by DSD Creative Group, Inc.

TABLE OF CONTENTS

DEDICATION

This book is dedicated to the many talented, dedicated and creative educators and advocates who are working together to help prepare American youths to achieve personal success and contribute to our shared community and national prosperity. We are privileged to know you, to learn from you and to strive with you in common purpose.

FORWARD

As a school leader, you have undoubtedly been faced with the research about employment opportunities, read about the shortage of students entering STEM fields, and arrived at the realization that for your students to be competitive in this new economy, skills and knowledge related to STEM is essential regardless of their field of interest. As principal of a comprehensive neighborhood high school that transitioned to a school with a STEM focus, my administrative team and I spent several years prior to the change searching for the answer to my most important question at the time. What exactly is a STEM school? Seems simple enough, but to my surprise it was not.

At the time I began my search there was no "how-to" guide, no definitive answers, and no suggestions of best practice. The models that existed were highly selective, application-based schools. We were simply a neighborhood school that wanted to provide relevance to our students in this 21st century economy. When we began our journey, there was not a resource available for me to read to begin to understand what pursuing a STEM focus meant. The STEM Leader Guide would have been a great place to start and could have saved our significant time in the planning process. The author, Hans Meeder, weaves together the case studies from his on-site visits with practical and helpful advice for any educator interested in STEM education to grasp the complexities of the challenge. His understanding of this landscape makes him a credible voice on the interrelation between STEM, the Project Lead The Way Program and Career and Technical Education. Not only does the text provide a sound definition of what STEM is in practical terms, it provides strategies for developing a STEM culture in your school and the action steps to get you started.

After several years implementing and scaling STEM education throughout my school, developing capacity among new administrators to implement a building wide STEM focus remains a high priority. As important is providing a context for new teachers to understand the importance of their work integrating STEM content and skills into their classroom. Undoubtedly, new staff members begin with the same simple question that ignited our journey, what exactly is a STEM school? Luckily, we now have the answer. I will surely use *The STEM Leader Guide* as a must read for any new staff member on my team.

Lazaro Lopez
Principal, Wheeling High School
Wheeling, Illinois

INTRODUCTION

AMERICA'S STEM EDUCATION CHALLENGE

This is a book about schools and school leaders; it is **for** school leaders who are charged with improving their schools—and meeting **America's STEM Education Challenge.**

America's STEM challenge is twofold—first we need a broad citizenry and workforce that is competent in applying technology, understanding scientific principles, and using mathematical problem solving in the workplace and the home. Second, we also need a specialized STEM workforce for a vibrant innovation sector that can match scientific and technological breakthroughs with business models that commercialize these breakthroughs on a large scale.

The STEM Education Challenge is to align all aspects of our education system—from elementary education to postsecondary education––to help develop both kinds of individuals – those who have general STEM literacy and those who are STEM experts.

This book takes an in-depth look at one critical period during which students from approximately seventh grade through twelfth grade have the opportunity to explore STEM careers and subjects and set a trajectory for their future studies and work. In these pages, I share research that my firm conducted on nine middle and high schools that utilize specialized STEM programs in engineering, technology, and bioscience. In our research, we observed how leaders and teachers in these schools worked to build systemic approaches to inculcating STEM literacy in all students and also lay the foundation for some students to become STEM experts.

Although education advocates, policy leaders, foundations, and business sponsors all have a legitimate voice in arguing for education relating to STEM, it is the local education leader who must set a course of action. To act effectively, the leader needs to be well versed in the broad discourse about STEM education. That local leader needs to develop an informed opinion, and then decide which ideas and resources will advance his or her school in the right direction.

To help you get started, we will dig more deeply into the issue of STEM education and explore the following questions:

Question 1   *What is STEM?*

Question 2   *What is STEM education?*

Question 3   *What data underpin the*
                    STEM Education Challenge?

Question 4   *Why is STEM education so important*
                    to policymakers and advocates?

Question 5   *What should be the goals of STEM education?*

Question 6   *What are policy prescriptions being*
                    suggested to improve STEM education?

Question 7   *How is America already responding*
                    to the STEM challenge?

Question 8   *What is the role of the local*
                    STEM education leader?

QUESTION 1 • WHAT IS STEM?

STEM (an acronym for science, technology, engineering, and mathematics) is a term on the lips and in the minds of school administrators, teachers, education policymakers, and business leaders throughout the United States.

But STEM means many things to many people. For some, STEM is simply a short-hand reference to four subject areas that each have a distinct definition, but are inter-related in the "real-world." Before we focus on their inter-relatedness, we will take a look at a useful definition of the component parts of STEM provided in a report by the National Academy of Engineering.[1]

"Science is the study of the natural world, including the laws of nature associated with physics, chemistry, and biology and the treatment or application of facts, principles, concepts, or conventions associated with these disciplines. Science is both a body of knowledge that has been accumulated over time and a process scientific inquiry that generates new knowledge. Knowledge from science informs the engineering design process."

"Technology comprises the entire system of people and organizations, knowledge, processes, and devices that go into creating and operating technological artifacts. Throughout history humans have created technology to satisfy their wants and needs. Much of modern technology is a product of services of science and engineering, and technological tools are used in both fields."

"Engineering is both a body of knowledge about the design and creation of human made products and the process for solving problems. This process is designed under constraint. One constraint in engineering design is the laws of nature, or science. Other constraints include such things as time, money, available materials, ergonomics, environmental regulations, manufacturability, and reparability. Engineering utilizes concepts in science and mathematics as well as technological tools."

- **"Mathematics** is the study of patterns and relationships among quantities, numbers, and shapes. Specific branches of mathematics include arithmetic, geometry, algebra, trigonometry, and calculus. Mathematics is used in science and engineering."

Although understanding the individual components of STEM is a good starting point, the adage that the "whole is greater than the sum of its parts" is appropriate in our thinking about STEM. The term "STEM" serves as a proxy for the "innovation economy" -- the nexus of scientific discovery, innovations, and the commercialization of these innovations into products and business models that help the U.S. economy succeed in the global marketplace.

QUESTION 2 • WHAT IS STEM EDUCATION?

One of the key findings from our research is that successful STEM transformation happens when school leaders take the time to define what they mean by STEM education and to articulate the goals of STEM education in the specific context of their schools.

When my team conducted its research, we did not encounter a common definition of STEM education that was used across the schools that we studied. With as much attention as the acronym STEM receives, there is still no official definition of STEM education that educators use consistently to guide their efforts. But in the following paragraphs are two definitions that have been proffered and have slightly different takes on what STEM is.

First, the President's Council of Advisors on Science and Technology (PCAST) provides the following straightforward definition of STEM education. This definition is focused on the subject matter covered included in the term.

> "STEM education ... includes the subjects of mathematics, biology, chemistry, and physics, which have traditionally formed the core requirements of many state curricula at the K-12 level. In addition, the report includes other critical subjects, such as computer science, engineering, environmental science, and geology, with whose fundamental concepts K-12 students should be familiar. The report does not include the social and behavioral sciences, such as economics, anthropology, and sociology; while appropriately considered STEM fields at the undergraduate and graduate levels, they involve very different issues at the K-12 level."[2]

A second approach, approved by the Maryland Board of Education, goes beyond a focus on content and discusses the interdisciplinary approach to instruction and the development of problem-solving skills.

> "STEM education is an approach to teaching and learning that integrates the content and skills of science, technology, engineering, and mathematics. STEM Standards of Practice guide STEM instruction by defining the combination of behaviors, integrated with STEM content, which is expected of a proficient STEM student. These behaviors include engagement in inquiry, logical reasoning, collaboration, and investigation. The goal of STEM education is to prepare students for postsecondary study and the 21st century workforce."[3]

THE ELEMENTS OF STEM EDUCATION

Drawing from these definitions of STEM education, and from what we saw played out in the schools we studied, I suggest a definition of STEM education should generally include five elements: STEM subject knowledge, STEM thinking and reasoning skills, STEM instructional strategies, STEM career-specific knowledge and skills, and integrated STEM (iSTEM).

STEM SUBJECT KNOWLEDGE

The most basic approach to STEM education syncs with the definitions provided in the National Academy of Engineering and PCAST reports, whereas the acronym really represents the knowledge and skills found within each of the particular disciplines.

STEM THINKING AND REASONING SKILLS

STEM experts have a foundational knowledge of math, science, engineering, and technology principles, but they often apply that knowledge in unpredictable settings that require a set of thinking and reasoning skills that often are not encouraged in traditional math and science settings. Therefore, for some schools in our study, STEM became a proxy for so-called "21st century skills." In each of the processes for design, mathematical problem solving, and the scientific method, there are similarities in framing a problem or hypothesis, brainstorming possible solutions or approaches, testing a method, gathering data, and assessing results against the proposed method or hypothesis. Certain learning instructional techniques (which we call "active learning in the next paragraph) focus on helping students develop these thinking and reasoning skills, which go far beyond the basic ability to recall facts and use pre-established formulas with given sets of data.

STEM INSTRUCTIONAL STRATEGIES

STEM education might also be used as a term that describes certain instructional techniques, which could be gathered under the umbrella term of active learning. These instructional techniques (problem-based, project-based, inquiry-based, and challenge-based) lead the learning process with a scenario or challenge to inspire and engage the student and then allow the students to gather information toward solving the problem or challenge. These active learning techniques simulate the way individuals learn in the "real world" and, therefore, help students more readily develop thinking and reasoning skills that are associated with STEM expertise.

STEM CAREER-SPECIFIC KNOWLEDGE AND SKILLS

Another approach to STEM education focuses on teaching specific technology, techniques, and concepts relating to the application of STEM content with a heavy focus on a particular career setting— such as computer science, forensic investigations, health science careers, or engineering. In these career-focused settings, STEM content will vary depending on which career field is being taught. For example, although similar problem-solving techniques would be taught, content would look very different depending on whether the course was a civil engineering, computer science, or veterinary medicine course.

ISTEM [4] (INTEGRATED STEM)

In the workplace, individuals with different STEM specializations often collaborate on multidisciplinary teams. The concept of iSTEM attempts to mimic real-world settings by creating instructional connections between the silos of content to provide a more authentic and engaging learning experience. On an operational level, teachers pursuing iSTEM work together to review their curriculum expectations and identify opportunities to link content from one course with that of another. They may re-arrange the flow of items covered in their courses so instruction on those items happens concurrently. In some cases, they may "swap" instruction of content from one course to another course to avoid unnecessary duplication. They may also create joint projects that draw from several content areas to enable cross-course collaboration among students. This approach to iSTEM was demonstrated by several of the schools in the *STEM Schools Project* and, in 2012–13, was reviewed by the National Research Council.[5]

Perhaps, in the totality of these components of STEM, there lives a richer, more useful definition of STEM education. Here is a suggested definition.

STEM Education is a thoughtful, well-planned endeavor to:

- Develop among students a solid grasp of the fundamental concepts and knowledge underpinning the core disciplines of science, engineering, technology, and mathematics.

- Help students develop the problem-framing and problem-solving skills to apply STEM concepts to new and unexpected challenges.

- Inculcate an understanding of how the scientific method, engineering and design processes, the use of technology, and the application of mathematical principles intersect to create the innovations that improve the human condition.

- Apply a mix of teaching methodologies, including active learning strategies, to help students apply and deepen their understanding of the core knowledge and concepts within STEM.

- Develop in students an understanding of the world of careers, how STEM concepts and knowledge are applied in a wide variety of career settings, and how these careers can be accessed through postsecondary education, technical training, and work-based learning.

QUESTION 3 • WHAT DATA UNDERPIN THE STEM EDUCATION CHALLENGE?

Following is a compilation of statistics about STEM achievement at both the K–12 and postsecondary levels that is often cited in support for increasing attention to STEM achievement and inspiration among American youths. The calls to action regarding STEM education are buttressed by a regular flow of research that underpins four chief concerns about the current state of STEM education.

- *American students perform poorly on national assessments in math, reading, and science.*

- *American students fare poorly in head-to-head international comparisons.*

- *Too few minority students and female students are interested in pursuing STEM careers.*

- *Compared with the number of international students involved in STEM education, too few American students are pursuing postsecondary education toward STEM careers.*

INTERNATIONAL COMPARISONS OF STUDENT ACHIEVEMENT

The Trends in International Mathematics and Science Study (TIMSS) ranks U.S. fourth graders and eighth graders as being about average in math and science achievement among industrialized and rapidly industrializing countries. However, the science and mathematics ability of U.S. students in the fourth, eighth, and twelfth grades drops progressively, compared with students internationally, as the grade level of U.S. students increases.[6]

In the 2006 Programme for International Student Assessment (PISA), a test that measures students' ability to apply what they have learned in science and technology skills, U.S. 15-year-olds scored below most other nations tested, and from 2000 to 2006, the U.S. standing dropped in both math and science.[7]

TROUBLING MATH ACHIEVEMENT ON U.S. ASSESSMENTS

On the National Assessment of Educational Progress (NAEP), just 40 percent of fourth graders and 35 percent of eight graders show proficiency in mathematics and science. There has been significant progress since 2000, but large numbers of students remain at the basic and below-basic levels of achievement.[8]

GAPS IN STEM INTEREST AND ACHIEVEMENT CORRELATED TO GENDER AND ETHNICITY

There is large STEM interest and achievement gap in the United States, and there have been historic discriminatory barriers that have prevented women and minorities from entering some STEM professions. As a result, African Americans, Hispanics, Native Americans, and women are seriously underrepresented in many STEM fields, and this limits their participation in many well-paid, high-growth professions.[9] Evidence also suggests that many underrepresented students have been gravitating away from science and engineering and toward other professions.[10]

A gender gap persists -- not in STEM aptitude -- but in interest: Although girls earn high school mathematics and science credits at the same rate as boys and earn slightly higher grades in those classes,[11] girls choose STEM majors in college at a much lower rate than boys.[12]

Girls who are high achievers in mathematics in the United States are concentrated at a small number of high schools, which suggests that most girls with high ability to excel in the field are not doing so.[13]

TOO FEW U.S. BORN STUDENTS IN STEM HIGHER EDUCATION

Only about a third of bachelor's degrees earned in the United States are in a STEM field, compared with approximately 53 percent of first university degrees earned in China and 63 percent of those earned in Japan.[14]

More than half of the science and engineering graduate students in U.S. universities are from outside the United States,[15] and more than two-thirds of the engineers who receive Ph.D.'s from U.S. universities are not U.S. citizens.[16]

Some leaders of business and industry have expressed concern that other countries—particularly China—are outpacing the United States in the production of engineers. Although it is difficult to make comparisons because of differences in the methods of collecting data and differences in how engineers are defined, the trends are clear. The number of science and engineering bachelor's degrees awarded in the United States has increased gradually over the past fifteen years, and as of 2007 was slightly more than 485,000. In China, by contrast, the number of university degrees in science and engineering was more than 840,000, a doubling of the number of degrees awarded between 1998 and 2006.[17]

QUESTION 4 • WHY IS STEM EDUCATION SO IMPORTANT TO POLICYMAKERS AND ADVOCATES?

There is a strong consensus among business, education, and political leaders about the enormous benefits that scientific and technological advancements have played in the U.S. economy and in support of U.S. global leadership. In fact, economist Robert Solow received a Nobel Prize for his work that indicated that well over half of the growth in U.S. output during the first half of the twentieth century could be attributed to advancements in knowledge, particularly technology.[18] [19]

Hence, if the United States were to lose its scientific and technological leadership, this would portend the nation's loss of its global economic leadership.

The concern, of course, is not new. For many decades, American education reform has been viewed in the context of international threats to the United States and its way of life. In the Sputnik era, increasing math and science achievement was touted as a necessary response to the military, economic, and cultural threat posed by Soviet communism. In the early 1980s, with the issuance of the "Nation At Risk" report, educational excellence, with a strong emphasis on math and science achievement, was offered as a critical response to the economic threat being posed by the resurgent Japanese and German industrial economies.

In the current era of education reform, the need for math, science, and technological achievement has gained a new sense of urgency in response to increased globalization, particularly the rise of China and India as places to which both low-skilled and high-skilled U.S. jobs have migrated.

In recent years, a number of blue-ribbon panels have issued reports heralding the troubled future. For example, in the National Academies' 2007 report, *Rising Above the Gathering Storm*,[20] leaders of industry and the academic community explained that

> *The vitality of the United States' economy is derived in large part from the productivity of well-trained people and the steady stream of scientific and technical innovations they produce. Without high-quality, knowledge-intensive jobs and the innovative enterprises that lead to discovery and new technology, our economy will suffer and our people will face a lower standard of living.*

The Gathering Storm committee concluded the following:

> *Having reviewed trends in the United States and abroad, the committee is deeply concerned that the scientific and technological building blocks critical to our economic leadership are eroding at a time when many other nations are gathering strength.*

In 2010, PCAST released its report titled "Prepare and Inspire: K–12 Science, Technology, Engineering and Math (STEM) Education for America's Future."[21] The report states that

> *The Nation's future depends on our ability to educate today's students in science, technology, engineering, and mathematics (STEM). Despite the fact that many U.S. students excel in STEM, U.S. students as a whole perform poorly on international comparisons of mathematics and scientific proficiency. …*
> *We must seize this historic moment by making changes and investments to educate all students for a future in which science and technology will play a critical role in the lives of individuals and the prospects of nations.*

Most education, business and political leaders agree, that while American education is improving, that rate of improvement may not be enough to keep pace with the challenge of supplying a skilled and talented workforce that can maintain the United State's economic competitiveness.

QUESTION 5 • WHAT SHOULD BE THE GOAL OF STEM EDUCATION?

Finally, there is an important question about the end goals of STEM education. Is STEM about building the next generation of scientists and technologists, about building a broader acquisition of STEM literacy for all students, or about promoting greater social equity? Or is the goal of STEM education a mix of all three?

DEVELOPING STEM LITERACY

One part of the mission of education is to prepare our youths for eventual success in the workplace. Given this mission, we certainly need to ask to what degree are STEM knowledge and skills—use of technology, use of statistical analysis, problem framing, and problem solving—being infused into the workforce?

Another important part of education's mission is to develop responsible citizens capable of self-government. In thinking about STEM education, it is fair to ask: "To what degree is clear thinking about STEM-related issues—research on climate change, understanding and applying findings from medical research, guarding against cyber threats––already a part of carrying out the rights and responsibilities of modern citizenship?

Given the challenges of work and citizenship in a highly technological society, it is pretty clear that all U.S. residents need to achieve a higher level of STEM "literacy." This new STEM literacy allows individuals to adapt and grow in the modern workplace and exercise the rights and responsibilities of citizenship and family leadership.

So one goal of STEM education is to develop a core level of STEM literacy for all students.

FILLING THE STEM EXPERTISE PIPELINE

There is also a strong push to replenish the expert STEM workforce that is nearing retirement and to expand our cadre of STEM experts to fuel new fields of innovation.

If STEM reform is just about filling the pipeline of scientists, technologists, engineers, and mathematicians to replace those leaving STEM-intensive careers, then that challenge is much less daunting. Those jobs make up about 5 percent of the U.S. economy.[22] The National Science Board speculates, for example, that simply improving postsecondary retention of students already enrolling in postsecondary STEM programs would largely solve the projected shortfall of STEM experts.

But it is also worth asking how STEM knowledge and skills are also impacting other career paths that are not traditionally considered STEM professions. For example, some career paths, like sales and marketing in a health or technology field or guiding the financing of a start-up Internet technology firm, may not count as classic STEM professions but may still require a higher level of competence in science, technology, engineering, or math.

Another practical concern is that, within the variety of STEM disciplines, there is a wide spectrum of needed skills and aptitudes. For some professions, lab-based science is the prominent skills. In others, the engineering process is prominent. In others, they use mathematics for calculation and modeling. So real STEM careers do not demand that a worker be equally proficient in all aspects of science, technology, engineering, and mathematics. In fact, the National Science Board calls attention to an aptitude called "spatial reasoning," which is necessarily high for engineers and technologists. But individuals with strong spatial reasoning may actually underperform in the more classic math or science competencies. That is why the National Science Board recommends that more attention be paid to assessing spatial reasoning and valuing it as a valuable skill on par with math and science competencies.

These factors indicate that while, on the aggregate, the United States and its students need to improve their STEM achievement, there is not a one-size-fits-all expectation of what that improved achievement should look like.

Earlier, we noted that about one third of U.S. college students are enrolled in a STEM postsecondary program, while that percentage is closer to 50 percent among Chinese and Japanese postsecondary students. With a growing definition of STEM expertise and STEM-enabled careers in the U.S. economy, school leaders might set a reasonable goal of cultivating about half of their student body toward a STEM expert pathway. Of course, not every student will or needs ultimately pursue a STEM expertise career path, but it would be excellent if half of U.S. youths had the reasonable preparation to pursue such a STEM pathway.

A final question in this discussion of STEM expertise is: How much of STEM talent is completely innate, and how much can be developed through good instruction, guidance and inspiration. There is no easy answer to this question, but it is worth having an open discussion within your school and identifying your educational philosophy with regard to this question.

PROMOTING SOCIAL EQUITY

An additional consideration for STEM education is whether moving more underrepresented students into pathways for STEM expertise can help address and ameliorate social disparities?

As a result of America's history of race and gender discrimination, there is a large gender and ethnic disparity between the current STEM workforce and the general population. This raises serious concerns about social equity and also about filling the future pipeline of STEM professions because the United States continues to evolve demographically.

Looking back to the Sputnik era when America tried to re-assert its preeminence in math, science, and technology, the goals of the math/science movement were explicitly focused on developing an elite core of scientists and technologists to underpin our national innovation infrastructure; the goal was to win the international space race to prove the superior benefits of free enterprise and democratic freedom.

There was no serious attention paid to developing STEM literacy among the general student population or to promoting social equity. Due to prevalent racial, ethnic and gender pre-suppositions, there was no real attempt to unlock the innate STEM talent in minority populations or young women.

Today's environment is very different. Population forecasts indicate that the majority of the U.S. population will be non-Caucasian by 2050, if not sooner.[23] Therefore, in order for the United States to realize greater overall prosperity, we need greater social mobility for economically struggling students, blacks, and Hispanics. Cultivating and supporting a diverse range of students into STEM education and helping them to enter STEM professions is not just a moral issue, it is an economic issue.

Given past inequities, perhaps minorities and women should be over-represented in future recruiting efforts. The end-goal is a population of STEM experts that mirrors the overall make-up of the U.S. population.

At a minimum, a worthy goal at the school level would be to create the personal invitations, challenges, and academic and social supports needed to ensure the enrollment of students in STEM expert courses. We need to develop every ounce of potential for STEM expertise, and STEM classes should not be primarily comprised of white males and Asian students.

THE LITERACY-EXPERTISE-EQUITY EQUATION

So let's agree that the goal for STEM education is a mix of three subgoals:

- **Build** STEM literacy among all students;

- **Cultivate** interest and talent to launch a significant percentage of students toward STEM expert careers; and

- **Create** a safe and challenging environment to attract students into STEM expert pathways who otherwise might have been left behind.

QUESTION 6 • WHAT POLICY PRESCRIPTIONS ARE BEING PROPOSED TO IMPROVE STEM EDUCATION?

As noted earlier, a number of national committees—such as the National Research Council, PCAST, and the National Science Board (part of the National Science Foundation)—have issued reports and made extensive recommendations related to STEM education. Most of these action steps are focused at the national or state policy level, and except for the first recommendation, have little applicability for the local education leader.

Still, as a STEM leader, you need to know what actions these entities are proposing, so that you can identify trends and opportunities to strengthen your STEM agenda. Among the many recommendations in these reports, some of the most significant to STEM education are:

Focus simultaneously on preparation and inspiration to achieve multiple goals for STEM Education. The PCAST committee said that, "to meet our needs for a STEM-capable citizenry, a STEM-proficient workforce, and future STEM experts, the Nation must focus on two complementary goals: We must prepare all students, including girls and minorities who are underrepresented in these fields, to be proficient in STEM subjects. And we must inspire all students to learn STEM and, in the process, motivate many of them to pursue STEM careers."[24]

Scale Up STEM specialty Schools. The PCAST report recommended creating up to 1,000 STEM specialty schools (from the current estimate of 100) during the decade between 2012 and 2022.[25] In the Gathering Storm report, to support the recommended action relating to STEM Advanced Placement (AP) and International Baccalaureate (IB) courses, the committee recommended expanded use of "statewide specialty high schools that would foster leaders in science, technology, and mathematics."[26]

Support Implementation of New National Math & Science Standards and Assessments. The Common Core State Standards are a set of English language arts and mathematics standards that were developed with input from educators, postsecondary faculty, and business with the guidance of the National Governors Association and the Council of Chief State School Officers, and they have been adopted by 45 states.[27] Another initiative is afoot, led by the National Research Council, the National Science Teachers Association, the American Association for the Advancement of Science, and Achieve, to develop the Next Generation Science Standards.[28] Both of these efforts are attempts to create common expectations for education across the nation and to raise the level of standards to that of the highest internationally performing educational systems. Two organizations are developing assessments that are aligned to the Common Core State Standards; states will be free to develop assessments aligned to the Next Generation Science Standards, but no cross-state effort has emerged as yet related to science assessment.

Recruit New STEM Teachers. The PCAST recommended "recruiting 100,000 high quality STEM teachers." Part of this recommendation makes reference to professional development of existing teachers.[29] The Gathering Storm committee established the goal to "annually recruit 10,000 science and mathematics teachers by awarding 4-year scholarships and thereby educating 10 million minds (over the career of these 10,000 teachers)."[30]

Help STEM Teachers Improve. The Gathering Storm committee recommended to strengthen the skills of 250,000 teachers through training and education programs at summer institutes, in master's programs, and in AP and IB training programs.[31]

Expand STEM AP and IB Course-taking. The Gathering Storm committee recommended to "Enlarge the pipeline of students who are prepared to enter college and graduate with a degree in science, engineering, or mathematics by increasing the number of students who pass AP and IB science and mathematics courses."[32]

Develop New Accountability Measures to Focus on Serving Upper-Tier STEM Students. The National Science Board called for policy that would "hold schools and perhaps districts and states, accountable for the performance of the very top students at each grade. Progress should be monitored for the top 10 percent and top 1 percent of students in each school using assessments than can adequately measure their performance."[33]

Provide Support for Effective STEM Programs (Both In-School and Out-of-School). The National Science Board also called for funding to "provide Federal support to formal and informal programs that have a proven record of accomplishment in stimulating potential STEM innovators. These should include formal education programs that use innovative teaching, methods or employ inquiry-based learning, and informal programs, such as robotics and invention competitions, Math Circles, hands-on 'lab days', mentoring opportunities, and science fairs." [34]

Recognize Spatial Talent in the Work of STEM Education.
The National Science Board suggested a policy that would
"expand existing talent assessment tests and identification strategies
to the three primary abilities (quantitative/mathematical, verbal, and
spatial) so that spatial talent is not neglected."[35]

QUESTION 7 • HOW IS AMERICA ALREADY RESPONDING TO THE STEM EDUCATION CHALLENGE?

As you know, myriad STEM school networks, education advocates,
and business-led organizations are hard at work to develop and
promote a STEM agenda. In this section, we provide information
about these organizations and trends, and give a nod to some
encouraging progress.

Classroom-Based STEM Curriculum. During the last two
decades, thousands of elementary, middle, and high schools
have launched a myriad of STEM programs, including branded
programs in engineering, biomedical sciences, and technology
from Project Lead the Way; Engineering is Elementary;
information technology programs authored by Microsoft, Cisco,
Oracle, and the Computing Technology Industry Association
of America (CompTIA); and information technology and
engineering academies offered through the National Academy
Foundation. Programs to strengthen STEM teaching include
UTeach and the Intel Math Program.

Extra-Curricular STEM Programs. A host of extracurricular
activities to engage students in competitions, expositions of
talent and knowledge, and real-world learning have blossomed.
Among dozens of opportunities are initiatives such as BEST
Robotics, FIRST Robotics, Honeywell/SAE Student Automotive
Design Challenge, Intel Science Talent Search, Lego Design
Challenge, Maker Faire, Merck Institute for Science Education,
Read World Design Challenge, Starbase 2.0, TechBridge, and
VEX Robotics.

STEM Education Networks. In 2012, approximately thirteen statewide networks of STEM educators came together to form the STEMx network.[36] As of mid 2013, the number of members had risen to nineteen and included Arizona, California, Colorado, Georgia, Idaho, Indiana, Kentucky, Michigan, New Mexico, New York, North Carolina, Ohio, Oklahoma, Oregon, Pennsylvania, Tennessee, Texas, Washington, and Washington, D.C.

National STEM Commissions. Several national reports, many of them referenced earlier in this chapter, have taken up the call to improve student achievement in STEM subjects by increasing the number of qualified math and science instructors, increasing the supply of specialty STEM schools, and attracting more young women and minorities into STEM fields of study.

STEM Business Coalition. In 2011, a national business coalition, Change the Equation,[37] was formed with corporate members that represented over 100 major U.S.-based and multinational corporations and a charge to better marshal corporate involvement in STEM education.

STEM-Focused Schools. During the first and second decades of the twenty-first century, dozens of STEM-focused schools have been and continue to be established, largely with support from national foundations and state and local funds set aside for specialty schools. Many of these initiatives have focused on creating new schools that specialize in STEM education, and many of these schools are relatively small, serving a few hundred students each.

National STEM Conference. To draw attention to STEM, in 2012, U.S. News and World Report sponsored a large national conference called STEM Solutions[38] that brought together hundreds of activists and change agents. Dozens of state STEM associations convene teachers and advocates across the nation.

STEM Achievement Improvements. Fortunately, not all the news about U.S. student achievement in STEM is bad. In fact, where there has been a concerted effort, improvements have occurred. For example, note the following:

Some individual states perform at relatively high levels. In Massachusetts, fourth graders score behind only two jurisdictions in math (Hong Kong and Singapore) and behind only one jurisdiction in science (Singapore).[39]

In Minnesota, the scores are only slightly lower. There are hints that participation in some STEM courses has increased. Since the late 1980s, the proportion of public high school seniors who graduate having taken at least one physics course has risen from less than 20 percent to 37 percent.[40]

Math test scores at the fourth and eighth grade levels have increased over the past two decades. On the NAEP for mathematics, the average fourth grade score rose from 213 to 241 between 1990 and 2011. For eighth graders, the average score rose from 263 to 284.[41]

Some of the achievement gaps between groups of students have narrowed. For example,

Hispanic and black students increased their mathematical performance between 2000 and 2007 and narrowed the gap between their performance and that of white students. The average score gap between black and white fourth graders shrank from 32 to 26 scale points between 1990 and 2007, and the average gap decreased from 2000 to 2007 between black and white eight graders after increasing between 1990 and 2000.[42]

The average score gap between black and white fourth graders shrank from 32 to 26 scale points between 1990 and 2007, and the average gap between black and white eighth graders decreased from 2000 to 2007 after increasing between 1990 and 2000.

QUESTION 8 • WHAT IS THE ROLE LOCAL STEM EDUCATION LEADER?

As we see from the array of activities and resources surveyed in this chapter, advocates, STEM teachers, education organizations, the philanthropic sector, government funders, researchers, and policy makers across the United States have been working intently to attract and motivate students to pursue the study of STEM fields and thus improve the competitiveness of the U.S. workforce.

But where do all of these STEM-focused reports, policies, funding initiatives, and curriculum offerings actually converge? For the most part, they converge at the local school and, in particular, in the classroom.

This means that local school leaders and teachers are the ones who must sift through all these ideas and resources, make some sense of the whole, and create a STEM agenda that works within the school. How this is done effectively—how local school leaders put together the pieces of the STEM puzzle—is the focus of the work our research team carried out. This is the research that will help you—the school leader or STEM coordinator—plan out a rational course of action and develop a STEM agenda that works for your school.

In the remainder of this book, we will look at schools we studied and what we discovered about the strategies that leaders use to design and implement a STEM school. After examining those strategies and examples from the schools themselves, I will share some key findings that emerged. Finally, I will lay out a series of action steps for you to consider at the local level (and also for leaders at state departments of education, national policy makers, and grant makers in education to consider).

So if you are ready to become a leader in building a STEM culture and you want to make this kind of impact on your school, please read on.

QUESTIONS FOR REFLECTION

- *Have I and my team defined STEM and STEM education?*

- *Can we articulate why STEM education important to our school and community?*

- *Have we gathered data that underpins our local STEM education challenge?*

- *What should be our goals for developing STEM literacy, cultivating STEM expertise, and enhancing social equity?*

- *Have we taken stock of STEM policies and programs already underway?*

- *What is my role as a school leader in addressing the STEM education challenge?*

CHAPTER 2

THE STEM SCHOOLS PROJECT

The purpose of the *STEM Schools Project*, carried out in 2011 and 2012, was to document promising practices in high schools and middle schools that provide students with a STEM-rich school experience by drawing upon a high-quality implementation of a STEM education program.

In our site visits and subsequent analysis, we asked two inter-related questions:

What factors contribute to a strong implementation of the STEM program?

and

How can a school move beyond having a good stand-alone STEM program to becoming a school that embeds STEM teaching and learning across the school—in short, a school that develops a STEM culture?

PROJECT LEAD THE WAY AND ITS IMPACT

With the backing of the Kern Family Foundation, we studied schools that were implementing one or more of the three Project Lead The Way (PLTW) programs. PLTW is a national, nonprofit organization that provides curriculum and teacher training for three STEM education programs: Pathway to Engineering (PTE; for high school students), Biomedical Sciences (BMS; for high school students), and Gateway to Technology (GTT; for middle school students). (For a listing of all PLTW course titles and abbreviations, see Appendix 1).

PLTW began in 1998 in 12 high schools in upstate New York as a program designed to address the shortage of engineering students at the college level. It has grown to a network of over 4,200 middle and high schools in 50 states and the District of Columbia. More than 500,000 students are enrolled in PLTW courses, and over 10,000 teachers have been trained.

The PLTW programs emphasize critical thinking, creativity, innovation, and real-world problem solving. According to the PLTW organization, "the hands-on, project-based program engages students on multiple levels, exposes them to areas of study that they may not typically pursue, and provides them with a foundation and proven path to college and career success in STEM-related fields."

One of the hallmark features of PLTW is the intensive two-week Core Training experience, during which a teacher receives preparation for the specific course they will teach, typically during the following school year. Teachers affectionately refer to this as a "boot camp" experience, one in which they receive an entire course overview and the opportunity to learn new technology and strengthen their knowledge of engineering, math, and science concepts that are embedded throughout the program. The Core Training is preceded by online readiness activities and then supplemented through ongoing web-based and live professional development opportunities.

PLTW was created "to address the country's need for more leaders in Science, Technology, Engineering and Mathematics (STEM)."[43] It has a clear workforce-related and competitiveness purpose.

PLTW courses certainly complement and reinforce core math and science courses offered in the school, but they are not designed to be a remedial-type intervention to help students make up for deficiencies in math, reading, and science knowledge.

A number of studies have looked at the impact of PLTW, and these are reviewed in a paper produced by Professor Robert H. Tai of the University of Virginia.[44] Tai's review concludes that "the strong, positive impact of PLTW on mathematics and science achievement as well as other important factors."

One study included in Tai's review clearly indicated that PLTW students were already farther ahead academically when they started the program, but that, when this initial bias was accounted for with matched comparisons, there was still a positive math and science impact correlated with PLTW. [45]Through an extensive review of student transcripts among Iowa students, this research found that students who participated in PLTW courses demonstrated a significant improvement in their math and science achievement over students who scored similarly at the eighth grade level but did not participate in PLTW. The PLTW students also took more math and science classes during high school, so it is difficult to determine whether the gain in math and science scores is attributed to PLTW courses they took, to the higher-level math and science courses, or both. It is also difficult to know whether these students are just "wired" to enjoy math and science more, or whether the PLTW courses, through their more creative and hands-on approach, reinforced an enjoyment of math and science that increased motivation, which transferred over to more traditional academic math and science courses.

Even with these unknowns, research indicates that, on the whole, PLTW students do as well as, or better than, non-PLTW students in science and math achievement.

During the course of our research, I observed about two dozen PLTW classes and I can attest that the project-based approach PLTW engages students in learning. Through the challenge of creative application of knowledge, students gain a deeper understanding of the relevant math and science concepts presented. This is the kind of learning that our research team observed among hundreds of young men and women. Although we tried to maintain our role as critical observers, frankly, we were very excited by what we saw.

STUDY DESIGN

In the *STEM Schools Project*, our research team wanted to identify a set of schools that represent the spectrum of schools that utilize Project Lead the Way, not just high-poverty, high-minority schools that are the subject of much education research. We gathered recommendations from regional consultants in the PLTW network to identify schools that were considered to be doing a good job implementing their current PLTW programs. These recommendations were based on program certification site visits conducted by the PLTW consultants. Next, we conducted structured phone interviews with leadership team members from these schools to discuss implementation of PLTW and efforts they were making to adopt broader STEM strategies. The team then selected nine sites—seven high schools, one middle school, and an intermediate unit school district—to visit during the fall of 2011.

The purpose of the site visits was to:

Meet with school leaders, teachers, students, business/community partners, and education partners to learn about their perspectives on key issues related to student achievement, student learning, PLTW, and STEM learning;

Develop an understanding of the school structure and curriculum;

Document the promising general school-improvement and STEM-specific practices in place at the school; and

Gather curriculum materials and data to document STEM integration and the development of higher-level skills of problem solving, analysis and synthesis, innovation, and teamwork.

The site visits generally occurred over two days. During the visits, two consultants from Meeder Consulting met with and interviewed key stakeholders associated with the schools (such as teachers, administrators, students, and business partners), observed PLTW and STEM classes, and reviewed school data and documentation. To structure the site visits, we developed interview questions for each group of stakeholders with whom we met. The questions focused on both school-level and district-level considerations. They also addressed the extent to which practices and policies were formal and driven by leadership, or whether practices were more informal and primarily teacher-driven. The interview questions focused on key themes related to PLTW implementation, STEM-related learning, and general school-improvement strategies.

In the months after the site visits, the research team conducted follow-up calls with representatives from the schools and collected additional documentation. For each of the sites, we prepared a detailed but reader-friendly report describing the school's accomplishments, approach to STEM learning, and school-improvement strategies. These case studies were released in June 2012 and were made available to the public through the Meeder Consulting website (www.meederconsulting.com). In addition, I shared our findings at a meeting of the National Engineering Council and National Research Council's Committee on Integrated STEM Education.[46]

THE SCHOOLS WE STUDIED

On the following pages, you can review charts that summarize basic information about each study site, followed by short profiles. Each profile explains how the site launched its PLTW implementation and how, in some cases, built a broader approach to STEM education.

SITE / LOCATION	SETTING	DEMOGRAPHICS	PLTW PROGRAMS OFFERED (SEE APPENDIX 1 FOR ABBREVIATIONS)
Clearbrook-Gonvick School Clearbrook, Minnesota	Rural	450 students (K–grade 12) White: 78% Native American: 18% Asian: 2% Others: 2% Free & Reduced Lunch (FRL): 45%	GTT PTE BMS
Edison Middle School Janesville, Wisconsin	Small city	670 students (grades 6–8) White: 75% Hispanic: 13% Black: 5% Asian: 3% American Indian: Less than 1% Other: 3% Special Education (SPED): 13% FRL: 59%	GTT
Greenfield-Central High School Greenfield, Indiana	Suburb of Indianapolis	1400 students (grades 9–12) White: 95% Hispanic: 2% Black and Asian: 3% SPED: 16% FRL: 27%	PTE BMS
Humboldt High School Humboldt, Iowa	Rural town	450 students (grades 9–12) White: 93% Hispanic: 4% American Indian/Alaskan 2% SPED: 9% FRL: 27%	PTE

SITE / LOCATION	SETTING	DEMOGRAPHICS	PLTW PROGRAMS OFFERED (SEE APPENDIX 1 FOR ABBREVIATIONS)
Lenawee Intermediate School District Adrian, Michigan	Rural, small towns	16,300 students (across 11 districts) White: 82% Hispanic: 12% Black: 3% Asian: 1% American Indian/Alaskan/other: 2% SPED: 12% FRL: 43%	GTT PTE
Pine River-Backus School Pine River, Minnesota	Rural town	White: 75% Hispanic: 13% Black: 5% Asian: 3% American Indian: Less than 1% Other: 3% SPED: 13% FRL: 59%	GTT PTE
Saint Thomas More High School Milwaukee, Wisconsin	Urban	440 students (grades 9–12) White: 59% Hispanic: 28% Black: 4% Asian: 3% American Indian/Alaska: 5 SPED: N/A FRL: N/A	PTE BMS
Wheeling High School Wheeling, Illinois	Suburban/ urban	White: 40% Hispanic: 49% Black: 2.5% Asian: 6% American Indian/Pacific Islander: 2.5% SPED: 16% FRL: 38%	PTE

CLEARBROOK-GONVICK SCHOOL • CLEARBROOK, MINNESOTA

Clearbrook-Gonvick School (CGS) is located in the town of Clearbrook, Minnesota, a rural town in the north-central part of the state that is home to 531 residents as of the 2000 census. CGS developed into a unified K–12 school as a result of numerous consolidations of single school districts during the 20th century. The school enrolls approximately 450 students, and the school's ethnic makeup is approximately 78 percent white, 18 percent Native American, 2 percent Asian, and the remainder other races. Approximately 62 percent of the elementary students and 45 percent of students in grades seven through 12 are eligible for Free and Reduced Lunch.

Despite being located in a very small, rural setting and facing significant financial challenges, CGS has built and maintained an intensive offering of technology, engineering, and biomedical opportunities for students. The district has also adopted an innovative blended curriculum that satisfies some state science requirements using PLTW course content.

As the district's single K–12 school, CGS delivers a comprehensive engineering and technology experience to all students in grades six, seven, and eight by making the GTT program required coursework. The school also offers a ninth grade physical science requirement that is fully integrated with PLTW's Principles of Engineering (POE) course and supplemented with chemistry instruction.

The school, which operates on a four-day-a-week basis because of severe budget constraints, also provides students with additional STEM learning opportunities during a voluntary Monday session offered at the school. Monday offerings include courses such as digital media, digital imagery, and robotics.

EDISON MIDDLE SCHOOL • JANESVILLE, WISCONSIN

Established in 1971, Edison Middle School is one of three middle schools serving the City of Janesville school district in southern

Wisconsin. Edison enrolls approximately 670 students in grades six through eight and serves students from both an urban area and a suburban geographic area. Approximately 75 percent of Edison students are white, 13 percent are Hispanic, 5 percent are black, 3 percent are Asian, 3 percent are "other," and less than 1 percent are American Indian/Alaskan. Thirteen percent of students receive special education services. Reflective of the changing community in which Edison students live, the demographics of the school's population recently experienced a pronounced shift. From 2000 to 2010, the percentage of Edison students who received Free and Reduced Lunch increased from approximately 27 percent to 59 percent. In addition, the percentage of Hispanic students enrolled at Edison almost doubled between 2006 and 2011.

Educators at Edison Middle School have created an integrated STEM experience for all seventh and eighth grade middle school students by fully integrating the GTT program with seventh and eighth grade math and science classes and eighth grade technology education (Tech Ed) classes. By providing support to the math, science, and Tech Ed teachers to collaboratively develop an integrated STEM experience, rather than offering GTT as a stand-alone program, the school is developing a school culture that emphasizes the value of STEM-related learning for every student. Furthermore, the district is creating a robust pipeline of students who are prepared to further their STEM focus in high school. With sustained district leadership, Edison and the other schools in the Janesville School District are implementing integrated GTT/STEM programs and also working to re-energize PLTW's PTE program at the high school level. The district leadership is also fostering a regional partnership of districts in Rock County that are pursuing related STEM strategies.

GREENFIELD-CENTRAL HIGH SCHOOL • GREENFIELD, INDIANA

Established in 1969, Greenfield-Central High School (GCHS) is a relatively large public high school located in the middle of Greenfield, Indiana, a suburban community about 15 miles east of Indianapolis. GCHS offers a full academic curriculum to students from the

Greenfield-Central school district. Approximately 1,400 students in grades nine through 12 attend Greenfield. Of the students enrolled at GCHS, 95 percent are white, 2 percent are Hispanic, and the remaining 3 percent are black or Asian. Approximately 27 percent of the students receive Free and Reduced Lunch, and 16 percent of the students receive special education services.

GCHS has achieved an exceptional level of student participation in courses related to STEM, with approximately one-third of its students participating in PLTW's PTE and BMS programs, as well as technology education programs. A large, cohesive team of math, science, and technology education instructors provide instruction in the PLTW courses, and the programs are highly valued by parents and business partners who see the programs as providing students with a high-quality preparation for future STEM-focused learning. GCHS enrolls a large percentage of students (about 50 percent) in one or more of its PLTW and technology programs.

HUMBOLDT HIGH SCHOOL • HUMBOLDT, IOWA

Humboldt High School is located in the north-central Iowa town of Humboldt, which lies approximately 110 miles northwest of Des Moines. Humboldt High School enrolls approximately 450 students in grades nine through 12. The school is the sole high school in the Humboldt Community School District. The district encompasses 200 square miles and includes the communities of Humboldt, Hardy, Dakota City, Renwick, Rutland, and Unique. (As of the 2011–2012 school year, Humboldt High School began enrolling students from a small neighboring school district.) Of the students who attend Humboldt High School, approximately 93 percent are white, 4 percent are Hispanic, and 2 percent are American Indian/Alaskan. Twenty-seven percent of students receive Free and Reduced Lunch, and 9 percent receive special education services.

As the home to a small rural high school, the Humboldt Community School District made a significant commitment to offering a sequence of PLTW PTE courses, several of which also offer dual-enrollment postsecondary credits. Teachers in the school district are working collaboratively to improve their teaching and curriculum and have laid the groundwork for additional collaboration and closer connections between PLTW courses and other courses that fall on the STEM spectrum.

LENAWEE INTERMEDIATE SCHOOL DISTRICT • ADRIAN, MICHIGAN

Located in Lenawee County, Michigan, approximately 70 miles southwest of Detroit, the Lenawee Intermediate School District (LISD) is a regional educational service agency that provides educational leadership and support services to the county's 11 local school districts. Lenawee County is approximately 760 square miles and has a population of approximately 100,000 residents. The LISD serves a total of approximately 16,300 students, of whom 82 percent are white, 3 percent are black, 1 percent are Asian, 12 percent are Hispanic, and the remaining 2 percent are American Indian/Alaskan or of "other" (multiracial) origin. Approximately 43 percent of the students receive Free and Reduced Lunch, and 12 percent of the students receive special education services.

The LISD leadership team is driving a district-wide approach to implementing PLTW in middle and high schools and to fostering a learning culture centered on STEM. The LISD aims to support all schools in using inquiry-based learning strategies that emphasize problem solving, project-based learning, and collaborative learning to prepare students for successful transitions to postsecondary education and careers. To help achieve this goal, the LISD provides opportunities for students to participate in STEM-related learning experiences beginning when they are in elementary school (through the Engineering is Elementary program[47]) and continuing through high school.

PINE RIVER-BACKUS SCHOOL • PINE RIVER, MINNESOTA

Pine River-Backus School (PRB) is located in Pine River in the heart of northern Minnesota's lakes and forest region. There are almost 7,200 residents within the district. The school serves elementary, middle, and high school students in one facility and enrolls approximately

950 students. There are fluctuations in the size of the senior class and attrition from one year to the next. The 2011–2012 class graduated 58 students. In the past, there have been classes of 70 seniors. The school population is predominately white, and about 70 percent of students receive Free and Reduced Lunch. Approximately 18 percent of students receive special education services.

PRB is a small school that provides an intensive offering of engineering technology opportunities for students and also has adopted an innovative blended curriculum that satisfies state science requirements with PLTW course content. The school delivers a comprehensive engineering and technology experience to all students in grades six, seven, and eight by making the GTT program required coursework. All students in grade nine participate in a GTT robotics course. Furthermore, the state's ninth grade earth science requirements are fully satisfied by the integration of chemistry instruction and content from PLTW's POE course.

SAINT THOMAS MORE HIGH SCHOOL • MILWAUKEE, WISCONSIN

Saint Thomas More High School (STM) is a private Catholic high school located in urban Milwaukee. The school building dates back 140 years to when it housed a seminary. Founded in 1972 as an all-boy, private high school, STM became a coed high school in 1989. About 440 students attend grades nine through 12. Approximately 59 percent of STM students are white, 28 percent are Hispanic, 5 percent are American Indian/Alaskan, 4 percent are black, and 3 percent are Asian.

STM offers both the PLTW BMS program and the PTE program, and approximately 50 percent of the student population enrolls in a PLTW course. The impact of PLTW on the instructional culture is growing. Several of the math and science instructors at the school already implement the project- and inquiry-based instructional approach used in PLTW. Individually, some teachers have taken the initiative to develop cross-curricular learning units. Both through its implementation of PLTW and its commitment to providing all students with innovative and rich learning experiences, STM is making strides in creating a culture of learning that values STEM.

WHEELING HIGH SCHOOL • WHEELING, ILLINOIS

Originally established in 1964, Wheeling High School (WHS) has redefined itself as a STEM-focused, comprehensive public high school. Wheeling, Illinois, is a suburban community located 28 miles northwest of downtown Chicago and has approximately 40,000 residents. The student population at WHS is ethnically diverse. Approximately 40 percent of students are white, 49 percent are Hispanic, 2.5 percent are black, 6 percent are Asian, and 2.5 percent are American Indian or Pacific Islander. Approximately 38 percent of the students receive Free and Reduced Lunch, and 16 percent of the students receive special education services. Wheeling's efforts at STEM education are built upon a solid foundation of PLTW's PTE program and a more recent advanced manufacturing program that was developed at the behest of PLTW's employer advisory committee. The leadership team and instructional faculty at WHS strive to equip all students, regardless of their education level or area of study, with a solid foundation of STEM knowledge. To support this STEM-for-all approach, learning activities at WHS are driven by the school-wide goal of "preparing students to think critically and solve complex problems, adapt to new technologies, and communicate effectively to a variety of audiences – all skills required to succeed in a global 21st century economy." Using an inquiry-based approach to instruction, teachers help students learn how to solve problems through investigation and how to purposefully link their learning across multiple disciplines. They teach and reinforce STEM-related skills, such as problem solving, teamwork, technology, and communication in all classes.

THOMAS WORTHINGTON HIGH SCHOOL • WORTHINGTON, OHIO

Located in Worthington, a suburb northwest of Columbus, Thomas Worthington High School (TWHS) is one of three high schools that serve the Worthington School District. TWHS, which is the oldest secondary school in Ohio and was the original high school in Worthington, enrolls approximately 1,500 students in grades nine through 12. Of the students enrolled at TWHS, 74 percent are white, 11 percent are black, 7 percent are Asian, 4 percent are

Hispanic, and the remaining 5 percent are American Indian/Alaskan or of "other" (multiracial) origin. Approximately 33 percent of the students receive Free and Reduced Lunch, and 11 percent of the students receive special education services.

At TWHS, a number of teachers from the disciplines of math, science, engineering, and technology education actively collaborate to create an integrated STEM learning experience for their students. With the encouragement of school administrators, this group of teachers creates cross-walks of their respective curricula, visit and observe other classes regularly, and offer students lessons and activities that explicitly link subject matters across multiple classes and previously discrete disciplines.

Students enrolled in the "STEM Academy" program experience science, technology, engineering, and mathematics as integrated and connected aspects of an overarching STEM education rather than as purely distinct subjects. Connecting across the STEM silos is not yet the norm for all teachers, but for a growing number of math, science, engineering, and other teachers, it is becoming a more pervasive approach to delivering their curriculum each progressive year.

REFLECTION QUESTIONS

- *Do any of the sites profiled in this chapter look similar my school or district, and could we learn from their experience?*

- *Have we already launched a specialty STEM program around which to develop a STEM culture?*

- *Have we done any work to integrate or create curricular connections among our STEM courses?*

Now that you know a bit about our research process and the schools we studied, I want to share our findings related to our two questions—how to offer a high-quality STEM program implementation and how to create a STEM culture.

CHAPTER 3

DEVELOPING A SCHOOL-WIDE STEM CULTURE

As our research team framed the site visit interview questions and then later analyzed the information we gathered from the site visits, *we organized our findings into three categories:*

The first category focuses on school-improvement practices; these practices are the "operating system" upon which individual STEM programs could be implemented and from which the school could move coherently toward developing a shared STEM culture.

The second category focuses specifically on what it took to implement the specialty STEM program (PLTW) to a high level of fidelity.

The third category focuses on the strategies that help build a strong STEM culture throughout the school.

BUILDING A STRONG SCHOOL-IMPROVEMENT INFRASTRUCTURE

When we visited sites that were part of the *STEM Schools Project* study, we asked our hosts a number of questions that extended beyond how they were working to implement their specialty STEM program(s) or their efforts to build a broader STEM culture. Not surprisingly, we found that these schools were moving toward their vision of success in STEM, and they were often simultaneously working to implement several general improvement strategies to help students experience learning success and help the school or district achieve other long-term goals. None of these strategies, whether they include specific programs or policies, exist in isolation within a school. They are interrelated and operate within the larger context of the school culture. For example, how the STEM program is implemented and how the program impacts student learning is affected by the policies, practices, and norms that define this culture. Improvement strategies often are implemented to help develop a strong organizational structure that supports and maximizes learning success for all students. They focus on adopting instructional approaches that meet the diverse needs of students, employing support services to help all students be successful, analyzing data to make instructional decisions, and providing teachers with relevant professional development.

An important issue to consider at the site level is the capacity to adapt to change. The sites we studied were already experiencing a measure of success in their implementation of PLTW, as well as working on broader school-improvement strategies. They had built enough momentum and positive culture inside the school whereby the specialty STEM program enhanced that positive momentum. In our study, we did not observe schools that were using their specialty STEM program to launch a turnaround strategy. It may be that some schools do not have enough capacity to implement a STEM program and rather should focus on building-block initiatives such as the ones listed in the following paragraphs.

Because the literature on school-improvement strategies is rich and the ground has been tilled many times, this section only includes a general discussion of five strategies we observed. But this does not suggest that these strategies are unimportant. In fact, I believe it would be foolish for a school to pursue a STEM agenda without having a strong school-improvement infrastructure.

This is where the original case studies will be useful. Readers can access the case studies at www.meederconsulting.com and review the detailed descriptions of the school-improvement strategies as well as how the schools implemented their specialty STEM programs.

KEY SCHOOL-IMPROVEMENT STRATEGIES

A. Provide Academic Support and Intervention to Enhance Student Learning. Schools provide targeted intervention services for students in need of additional academic and behavioral support. Such services may be implemented on an individual basis or for a group of students struggling with similar issues.

B. Offer Career Development and College Planning. To prepare students for a successful transition to postsecondary education leading to a career, the leadership team consistently provides students with guided planning for their post graduation pursuits. Such planning may include focused career exploration opportunities that recur and progress throughout a student's schooling and the development of long-term plans of study that extend beyond high school.

C. Offer the Opportunity to Earn College Credit. To help students transition successfully to postsecondary learning opportunity, the school provides students with opportunities to earn concurrent credit while still in high school and also to acquire advance credits through Advanced Placement and International Baccalaureate programs.

D. Focus on Professional Development, Growth, and Collaboration. The school leadership team supports professional development opportunities that are job-embedded, targeted, long term, and focused on collaborative learning.

E. Use Data to Make Instructional Decisions. To improve student performance, leadership and instructional teams analyze and use achievement data to drive instruction and identify students in need of additional academic support.

IMPLEMENTING A SPECIALTY STEM PROGRAM

We observed that district and school leaders needed to implement PLTW through a deliberate and well-thought-out process in order to maximize the benefits to students. A thorough implementation of PLTW harnesses the program's potential to serve as a springboard for larger-scale transformations in teaching and learning in the school and builds the sustainability and scalability of the program over time. To adopt this approach, leaders committed to a thorough implementation of PLTW, viewing PLTW as an integral part of the overall vision and culture of the school rather than as a mere add-on school program. Such an approach requires leaders to aggressively plan for how PLTW will be implemented over the long term, to build a sustainable pipeline of PLTW students, and to secure the support and buy-in of key stakeholders within the school and the community the school serves.

The following components were key to implementing a high-quality STEM program that could provide a foundation for a STEM culture:

A. Thoroughly Plan the STEM Implementation. Before a district or school moves forward in implementing a STEM program, the leadership team secures buy-in from key stakeholders, such as other administrators, instructors, and members of the business community. Part of the planning phase may involve convening a committee of interested stakeholders to gather information about the need for a program, plan for ongoing business and community involvement, secure financial resources, and garner advocacy within the community. Key stakeholders demonstrate a shared commitment to fully implementing the STEM program in order for the program to be initiated and sustained effectively over the long term.

B. Select and Support a Strong Instructional Team. Although the school leadership team can create an environment conducive to implementing a high-quality

PLTW program, ultimately it is the STEM program instructors who largely determine its success in terms of improving student engagement and learning. District and school leadership selected a team of instructors for the STEM program who possess a passion for instructional excellence and continuous professional growth and who thrive on collaborating with their peers. These instructors are willing to embrace project-based learning and dismiss the outdated notion of closing the door and teaching.

C. *Plan to Reach All (or Most) Students.* The most exceptional examples of how the STEM program is implemented across schools were found at those sites that committed to fully and thoroughly implementing the program for all (or most) students. At these sites, the STEM program is not considered to be an add-on to other curriculums or an elective for a small percentage of students who are already strongly attracted to STEM-related learning. Instead, the leadership team views the STEM program as an integral component of the school's program offerings and one that benefits most, if not all, students. The STEM program is fully ingrained in the culture of the school.

D. *Reach Out to Local Businesses to Gain and Sustain Support.* For students to experience the rich and deep potential of the STEM program as a program designed to make learning engaging and relevant for students, district and school leaders reach out to and engage local businesses in the program. This engagement extends beyond business representation on the advisory council (a requirement to earn PLTW program certification). A deeper level of engagement involves creating opportunities for students to interact often with professionals and observe and participate in real-world learning projects. Education leaders take the initiative to reach out personally to potential business partners, effectively communicate the mutual value the STEM program provides to students and the businesses, and outline specific partnership opportunities.

E. Reach out to prospective students. To develop a sustainable pipeline of students and to make the STEM program a defining presence in the school culture, district and school leaders conduct targeted outreach to prospective students. Outreach efforts focus on students at all grade levels, including elementary school students. These efforts include the sharing of general information about the STEM program, highlighting of the type of projects that PLTW students complete, and providing insight into how the program can prepare students for success beyond high school.

TAKING ACTION TO DEVELOP A SCHOOL-WIDE STEM CULTURE

In schools that develop a STEM culture, STEM-related learning strategically occurs across science, math, and PLTW courses through relevant and meaningful instructional approaches implemented by the teachers and driven by the school leadership team. The school team moves beyond offering stand-alone STEM-related opportunities to a select subset of students. Instead, it establishes policies and practices that provide all students with focused, sustained, and purposeful STEM-rich learning experiences.

These strategies are specifically directed to help move the entire school (or a significant portion of the school) to develop a comprehensive STEM focus, to take steps to help all students reach a basic level of STEM literacy, and to help another significant percentage of students to develop a STEM expertise.

The three overarching strategies to develop a school-wide STEM culture are as follows:

1. **Establish Shared Guiding Principles for STEM Learning.**
2. **Implement Innovative STEM Curriculum and Instruction.**
3. **Engage Math, Science, and PLTW Teachers in Collaborative Planning and Instruction.**

Each of the strategies also includes one or more substrategies. After the description, you will also see a "Strategy in Action" that show how the strategy played out in a specific study site.

STRATEGY 1 • ESTABLISH SHARED GUIDING PRINCIPLES FOR STEM LEARNING

In schools with a STEM-rich culture, the leadership team and instructional staff know which practices constitute STEM-related instruction, which skills and knowledge a student must possess to be considered STEM literate, and what STEM learning looks like in practice. Under this strategy of establishing shared guiding principles for STEM learning are three related but distinct substrategies: Define STEM Literacy, Define STEM Education, and Develop District-wide Vision for STEM Learning.

Substrategy 1A • Define Stem Literacy

The staff at schools with a STEM culture develop a shared understanding of STEM literacy in order to focus instructional decisions around integrating the related knowledge and skills throughout multiple disciplines, specifically math, science, and PLTW.

*The Strategy in Action**

*Note to reader: In each of these "The Strategy in Action" sections, the past tense is used to describe what the research team saw at the time of the site visits and in follow-up discussions. More than likely, most of these practices are still in place, but they may have evolved to some degree.

LENAWEE INTERMEDIATE SCHOOL DISTRICT

LISD administrators and staff actively worked to increase STEM literacy throughout the county. As part of this work, they defined STEM literacy as such: "STEM literacy means that a student possesses the ability to apply understanding of how the world works within and across the areas of science, technology, engineering, and math. STEM literacy is an interdisciplinary area of study that bridges the four areas. A STEM-literate student is also experienced in problem-solving, analytical, communication, and technology skills." [48]

Building from this STEM literacy definition, the STEM Advisory Committee, a committee charged with developing and overseeing a county-wide approach to STEM, worked to establish a set of STEM-specific knowledge and skills.

THOMAS WORTHINGTON HIGH SCHOOL

To clarify the instructional goals of its STEM pathways, the instructors at TWHS created a STEM Literacy Pyramid,[49] adapted from a presentation by faculty from the University of Maryland, to help define what skill sets and tools are important to developing STEM literacy. They also mapped out the commonalities among problem-solving processes, or the STEM processes, across math, science, and engineering. The following table illustrates those commonalities.

STEM PROCESSES		
ENGINEERING DESIGN PROCESS	**SCIENTIFIC METHOD PROCESS**	**MATHEMATICAL PROBLEM-SOLVING PROCESS**
• Identify the problem • Plan project • Problem Specifications • Conceptual Design • Final Design	• Ask & define the question • Gather information & resources through observation • Form a hypothesis • Perform one or more experiments, collect & sort data • Analyze the data • Interpret the data and make conclusions that point to a hypothesis • Formulate a "final" or "finished" hypothesis	• Read the problem • Identify and organize important information • Choose an appropriate strategy and/or formula • Solve the problem • Check your work

Substrategy 1B • Define STEM Education

At the time we conducted our site visits, there were not many readily available definitions of STEM education, such as the one I offered in the introduction section of this book. But the lack of a consistent definition did not negate the need for such a definition as a rallying point for school leaders and teachers and as point from which the school leaders and teachers could move forward. When it came to defining STEM education, many of the schools in our study were doing the proverbial "building the airplane while we're flying it." They wanted to move forward, but there was neither a clear definition of STEM education nor a blueprint for exactly what to do. Here is how they grappled with creating a definition of STEM education.

The Strategy in Action

WHEELING HIGH SCHOOL, WHEELING, ILLINOIS

Principal Laz Lopez arrived at WHS in 2007, three years after the PLTW implementation began. Although he recognized the great potential of PLTW, he was immediately struck by the increasing need to provide STEM-focused learning to *all* students, not just gifted or "techie" kids.

The WHS leadership team established a goal that every student would receive STEM-related content no matter what they choose to study. Regardless of whether a student participated in a traditional STEM course or a nontraditional STEM course, the STEM skill set was embedded and relevant to every student's school experience.

The WHS team stressed that the STEM-for-all approach was not an effort to create a career technical education program only for students who did not plan to attend a four-year college; rather, it was *meant to expose all students to the STEM skill set as it applied in all content areas, regardless of a student's planned postsecondary path.*

Through its STEM-for-all approach, WHS teachers were expected to pursue the school-wide goal of "preparing students to think critically and solve complex problems, adapt to new technologies, and communicate effectively to a variety of audiences – all skills required to succeed in a global 21st century economy." [50] Instructors taught and reinforced skills related to STEM, such as problem solving, teamwork, technology, and communication, in a broader context in all classes.

In accordance with the skills outlined by the Partnership for 21st Century Skills (P21)[51], every student was expected to develop the following skills, defined by WHS as "STEM skills."

PROBLEM SOLVING • TEAMWORK • TECHNOLOGY • COMMUNICATION

To bring this STEM-for-all approach to life, the teachers evaluated how STEM skills were being integrated into each course offered at WHS. On the basis of the skills outlined by P21, teachers aligned STEM-related skills content within their courses and highlighted reading materials with related STEM content. The P21 skills framework provided teachers with a tool to use in adapting these STEM skills to, and aligning them with, their curriculum.

Because becoming a STEM school was a new concept at WHS, the leadership team worked to provide consistent and varying types of professional development to the teachers. Teachers regularly collaborated with their professional learning team (PLT; a group of teachers in the same subject area) to brainstorm how an authentic research experience could occur. School leadership also regularly met with the heads of each PLT to further explore how to cultivate STEM literacy across all disciplines.

Over time, WHS incorporated all subject areas in an interdisciplinary approach, training students to transfer and apply knowledge and skills across the curricular spectrum rather than isolating each subject area. Teachers also consistently reinforced STEM literacy by embedding the QUEST model (described later in this section) in their classrooms.

Substrategy 1C • Develop District-wide Vision for STEM Learning

Because of the sense of urgency to address the STEM challenge, school and district leaders often want to get started quickly. Finding a comprehensive, well-structured program like PLTW makes that effort more feasible in a relatively short time frame. (See Appendix 1 for information on the courses offered through PLTW, and Appendix 2 for a sampling of other STEM classroom-based and extra-curricular programs.) But school and district leaders balance their desire for quick action with an effort to think long term about where they are headed with STEM education, envisioning what it will look like in the short and medium term. This planning effort is characterized by convening planning groups of educators and also organizing employer and community partners to give input to the school and district. It is also characterized by creating written plans that all stakeholders can view and to which the school and district holds itself accountable.

The Strategy in Action

LENAWEE INDEPENDENT SCHOOL DISTRICT

LISD administrators viewed STEM-based learning as an important component of a well-rounded education. Their goal was to increase students' exposure to STEM beginning at the earliest levels and continuing beyond graduation.

LISD leaders viewed PLTW as one of multiple opportunities to expose students to STEM-related courses, regardless of their future career path. To achieve their overall STEM education goals, they initiated several support mechanisms, including strong district-level support for STEM and STEM awareness activities. These district-level efforts were intended to promote STEM-related learning for all students in all district schools.

The LISD funded a full-time STEM Services Director to ensure that the LISD STEM Services mission "To improve K-12 teaching and learning in science, mathematics and technology and prepare students for higher education and science, technology, engineering, and mathematics careers in the 21st century" was carried out.

The STEM Services Director, who reported to the LISD Assistant Superintendent, played a pivotal role in the PLTW implementation process at the local districts. She oversaw the grants and helped districts create their implementation plans. In addition, she made sure that districts were meeting the requirements of the operational agreement. The STEM Services Director was the key point of contact between the LISD and the Lenawee County STEM Advisory Committee, a group of business representatives and educators who provided input on STEM education for the district. The STEM Services Director also collected and reported baseline data about STEM instruction, based on achievement data and study survey data, to gauge student interest in math and science in grades two through eight.

LISD administrators emphasized the importance of establishing an early awareness of, and interest in, STEM content and careers. To help achieve these goals, the LISD operated several youth summer programs focused on career exploration for the county's students in preschool through eighth grade. The cost of the camps was subsidized by the LISD, so the cost for participants was typically only $50–$100 for the full session. These camps were very popular, as evidenced by the fact that nearly 90 percent of the possible spaces for summer camps were filled. The preschool camp was 100 percent filled.

THOMAS WORTHINGTON HIGH SCHOOL

As of 2011, Worthington schools were beginning to develop a district-wide vision for STEM education. Working under direction of district leadership, a group of PLTW and STEM teachers, along with district curriculum leaders, were working collaboratively to define the STEM vision. One of the early working versions of the STEM vision statement read as follows:

> *"The vision for STEM education for Worthington City Schools is to engage students in a rigorous integrated PK-16 inquiry-based education that substantially increases the number of youth who*

possess not only the valuable skills of problem solving, logical thinking, and innovating, but who graduate from high school both college and career ready."

Although this vision statement had not yet been officially adopted by the Board of Education during the time that the study was conducted. It was expected to become part of the STEM graded course of study once that curriculum was approved in the next year.

STRATEGY 2 • IMPLEMENT INNOVATIVE STEM CURRICULUM AND INSTRUCTION

Under this strategy of implementing innovative STEM curriculum and instruction, there are two related but distinct substrategies: Integrate STEM-rich Instruction across Math, Science, and Other Applied STEM Programs and Implement Inquiry-based and Project-based Learning Strategies.

Substrategy 2A • Integrate STEM-rich Instruction Across Math, Science, and Other Applied STEM Programs

In schools with an established or developing STEM culture, students participate in learning experiences that connect across multiple disciplines, specifically math, science, and PLTW courses. These connected learning experiences reinforce and deepen their understanding and application of knowledge.

When connected instruction is implemented consistently and deliberatively, rather than in an ad hoc fashion, a true STEM culture is established and the learning connections are transparent for students. Students see that STEM content occurs in real-world contexts, and for many students, this context helps increase their motivation and their grasp of content.

The Strategy in Action

CLEARBROOK-GONVICK SCHOOL AND PINE RIVER-BACKUS SCHOOL

CGS and PRB implemented similar approaches to integrating STEM content. They both offered an integrated course that reflects both the content of PLTW's POE course and Minnesota's physical science standards. Because the state standards for ninth grade physical science significantly overlapped with the material offered in POE, it was possible to integrate the courses into one. However, the state's physical science standards also included a unit of chemistry content that needed to be incorporated.

Because incorporating the chemistry content took up most of the remaining instructional time left in the course, CGS asked the English department to supervise the research project component of the POE curriculum. All ninth graders took the POE/physical science class so the research component could be embedded into the ninth grade English classes.

EDISON MIDDLE SCHOOL

For seventh grade students at Edison, science and PLTW instruction were tightly linked. The seventh grade math/science instructional team purposefully integrated several PLTW units into the science curriculum and estimated that the GTT units account for approximately 60 percent of the curriculum they taught.

The level of integration between science and PLTW material was so deep that a classroom observer and most students were not able to differentiate between what was technically PLTW content and what was science content. Integration occurred seamlessly as students moved through science and PLTW learning activities interchangeably. For example, students concluded a science unit on simple machines by creating a Rube Goldberg machine (an example of a machine that performs a very simple task in a very complex fashion); this activity is officially part of the PLTW Science of Technology unit. The instructors emphasized that linking their instruction across science and PLTW allowed students to better understand the application of the lessons and skills they taught. They also stated that students made better connections across these content areas and saw "value in [what they learn] in school."

Prior to implementing the PLTW units, the teachers identified which units aligned with the science curriculum and how these units could replace some of the pre-existing curriculum and yet still address the same objectives. Once the formal alignment process was completed, the instructors continued to plan collaboratively each week to determine the pace of instruction and specific learning activities to implement.

SAINT THOMAS MORE HIGH SCHOOL

Much of the integration that occurred across math, science, and PLTW courses at STM was supported by the school leadership team, but admittedly, the school was still early in the implementation process.

In 2009, STM introduced the BMS program. While attending summer training for the program, an instructor realized that the content of STM's biology course was duplicative of the introductory course for PLTW's Principles of Biomedical Sciences (PBS) and much too traditional in style. Therefore, she initiated the development of a special biology course called Biomedical Sciences Biology. This new course was specifically designed to be taught concurrently with the PLTW PBS course. The customized biology course reinforced what was taught in PBS so that what the student learned in the biology course could be directly applied to was being learned in the PBS course. For example, when the students learned about the characteristics of bacteria cells in biology, they could see how that applied to the selection of antibiotics in PBS. Another added benefit of the two courses being taught concurrently was that some of the content needed in PBS could be covered in biology. As the PLTW instructor stated, "Instead of teaching the basics of DNA structure in PBS, we can teach that in biology and in PBS we have more time to work on the projects related to the structure."

In another example of cross-discipline collaboration, one math instructor spoke about coordinating the teaching of "best-fit lines" (the line that best represents the trend of a data set) with an STEM science teacher. This collaboration began when the two teachers co-taught a summer course, learned more about one another's courses, and began to observe shared content and opportunities for collaboration. In one instance, the two teachers worked together so that students performed calculations on data sets in the math class that had been generated and collected in a science class a month or two beforehand. Students were reminded that the data they were manipulating were the same data they previously generated; this helped them see the direct relevance of the data and also to understand that real-world data are not as perfect or consistent as data drawn from textbooks.

Similarly, the two teachers collaborated on the instruction related to conversions between advanced algebra and science related to "dimensional analysis," a concept that is covered in both their courses, albeit with slightly different terminology and procedures. To make the shared concept more consistent, the math class adopted the same terminology as the science course.

THOMAS WORTHINGTON HIGH SCHOOL

TWHS had a history of interdisciplinary planning, including participation in a district-wide Integrated Math initiative in the 1990s, which established an early math–technology connection. The integration of the PLTW program and the STEM School at TWHS provided a strong foundation to support the continued development of holistic STEM-based education.

As the first step for collaboration, which in TWHS's case was teacher-driven, the PLTW and academic teachers at TWHS began to build connections between their classes and to develop collaborative lesson plans. Through a curriculum-mapping process (where they "mapped" out the content that is covered in their class as well as the sequence in which content is delivered), teachers identified topics that they taught in common with other disciplines. They realized there were commonalities among some of the content but also that they teach different concepts at different points in the year. They did not try to change the sequence in which they taught content, but focused on drawing connections between the courses and making sure that students recognize those connections.

Examples of classes they have connected include:

- *Introduction to Engineering Design (IED) with Geometry, Algebra II, and Physical Earth Science Systems (PESS)*

- *POE with Physics, Algebra II/ Functions Statistics Trigonometry (FST), and Pre-Calculus Discrete Math (PDM)*

- *Digital Electronics with FST*

In one example of collaboration, the geometry teacher introduced students to the use of Inventor (software used in PLTW) at the beginning of the year as a tool to review geometry concepts. In his words, "I found that I was teaching concepts built into the Inventor program. By using Inventor for STEM geometry, students begin to make connections faster than I can in the classroom." This also benefited the IED teacher because students came to his class ready to use the software.

In another example, freshman STEM students designed and built miniature cars in the IED class. Once the cars were built, the science class students built a testing system to measure the acceleration of the cars. Data from the test runs of the cars were collected and put into an online spreadsheet for the POE class. The POE class used the data to create spreadsheets that calculate accelerations of the cars based on different sets of available data. This application helped students understand when to use certain kinematic equations versus other equations. The STEM Physics class also used the data to calculate forces and momentum created by the release of CO_2 from the cars.

After a small group of teachers had experimented with course-by-course curriculum mapping and collaboration, they sought permission to create a more structured approach through the creation of a "STEM School," what is essentially a small learning community.

The STEM School concept was first introduced in 2009 as a Small Learning Community (SLC) organized around science, technology, engineering, and math courses and linked to the PLTW engineering academy. Students who wished to pursue a STEM-based curriculum could choose to enroll in the PLTW engineering academy, the "STEM School," or both.

The STEM School was officially launched in the 2011–2012 school year, and TWHS had 64 students enrolled in the STEM pathway (27 in STEM POE, 18 in STEM IED, and 19 in STEM Digital Electronics (DE) during the study.

The following charts show the typical course schedule for students in the STEM School. There were two paths to accommodate students with varying levels of math preparation. The first chart represents the courses for students who entered the STEM program at the Geometry level. The second chart represents the path for students who entered at the Enriched Algebra II level. (Algebra I [commonly taken in a student's eighth grade year] is a prerequisite for the STEM School.)

Students who chose to participate in PLTW but not the STEM SLC signed up for their traditional math and science courses and then supplemented these courses with PLTW courses. However, many students chose to enroll in both PLTW and the STEM School, which allowed them to enroll in STEM science, STEM math, and STEM PTLW courses.

When the STEM School was up and running, Worthington teachers and administrators began working together to develop an official, integrated STEM curriculum for the district. They sought to develop STEM standards and planned to seek Board of Education approval for new graded courses of study for three STEM science classes.

Thomas Worthington High School • 2011-2012 STEM Pathway
STUDENTS ENTERING AT THE GEOMETRY LEVEL

	Grade 9	Grade 10	Grade 11	Grade 12
MATH	STEM Geometry	STEM Honors Algebra II	STEM FST (Functions Statistics Trigonometry)	STEM PDM (Pre-Calculus Discrete Math)
SCIENCE	STEM PESS (Physical Earth Science Systems)	BESS (Biological & Earth Systems Science) and STEM Physics	STEM Chemistry with Optional AP Courses	AP Courses or Postsecondary (dual enrollment courses)
PLTW	STEM IED	STEM POE	STEM DE (Possible Future CEA)	STEM Engineering Design and Development (EDD)

Thomas Worthington High School • 2011-2012 STEM Pathway
STUDENTS ENTERING AT THE HONORS ALGEBRA II LEVEL

	Grade 9	Grade 10	Grade 11	Grade 12
MATH	STEM Honors Algebra II	STEM Honors FST (pending dept. approval)	STEM Honors PDM	STEM Calculus or Postsecondary (dual enrollment courses)
SCIENCE	STEM PESS	BESS & STEM Physics	STEM Chemistry with Optional AP Courses	AP Courses or Postsecondary (dual enrollment courses)
PLTW	STEM IED	STEM POE	STEM DE (Possible Future CEA)	STEM EDD

Substrategy 2B • Implement Inquiry-based and Project-based Learning Strategies

Many STEM programs, including PLTW, are built upon an educational philosophy called "project-based learning." One definition of project-based learning (PBL) is "a systematic teaching method that engages students in learning essential knowledge and life-enhancing skills through an extended, student-influenced inquiry process structured around complex, authentic questions and carefully designed products and tasks."[52]

In the PBL approach, the projects are meant to engage students by cultivating their curiosity and creating challenges that help them develop their problem-solving skills. Inquiry-based learning is somewhat similar, but instead of a project, questions drive the learning process forward.

The project-based learning approach is already built into the PLTW curriculum, but it is not the norm in many other math and science classes. Schools that implement project-based and inquiry-based learning in other STEM classes typically rely on entrepreneurial and self-directed teachers to do the work. Some schools set specific expectations in this regard and provide professional development and time for teachers to do the work of revising their curriculum.

School leaders should be aware that, even for individual math or science teachers who teach a specialty STEM course that utilizes project-based learning, it is a bit of a pipe dream to think that teachers will just naturally evolve in the way they teach their other core STEM classes. Being trained to deliver a project-based curriculum like PLTW is very different from actually rewriting curriculum to utilize a project-based orientation. Changing curriculum and instructional approaches takes intensive time and effort, and in most cases, requires preliminary professional development and an ongoing supportive environment to keep up the momentum. We observed examples of entrepreneurial teachers who took this initiative, but we also saw many PLTW teachers who did not change the way they taught their core math and science classes.

The Strategy in Action
WHEELING HIGH SCHOOL

In 2010, WHS introduced a school-wide inquiry model framework (called QUEST) to drive instruction and teach students how to approach a problem and work through it. The model was created by the WHS leadership team, and was built upon problem-based learning by guiding students toward investigating each and every element within a problem. *QUEST comprised five elements:*

Question	*Identify the purpose of the audience*
Understand	*Use available resources to plan an appropriate course of action*
Evidence	*Collect and organize data from credible sources or experiments*
Synthesize	*Analyze results to draw conclusions and assess validity*
Tell	*Develop product to effectively communicate research and results to the identified audience*

In QUEST, instructors used a common framework and vocabulary to develop common skills among students. And whereas inquiry-based learning was often left to the science department, the WHS leadership team built capacity for all instructors to talk about it, teach it, and embed it in the culture so students became comfortable solving problems.

To further internalize the QUEST concept, all WHS students put the framework into practice by conducting original research based on a topic chosen by a team of teachers. One project consisted of students conducting a real-life inquiry project with a local Japanese grocer about the safety of food coming from Japan after the 2010 tsunami. Another project involved student teams examining issues and problems associated with obesity.

SAINT THOMAS MORE HIGH SCHOOL

Saint Thomas More High School (STM) was in many ways a traditional content-based teaching and learning environment. However, Curriculum coordinator Mary Burke recognized that the PLTW's learning strategies of inquiry and problem solving in this small school environment would promote a culture that encourages experimentation in other disciplines. Teachers in social science, theology, and English experimented with peer and cooperative learning structures and formative and varied assessments. Although the school's professional development program introduced the project-based instructional approach to other courses, the science department was the first to adopt the approach extensively, and project-based learning also began to make an impact on the math department.

One teacher who taught science (and later PLTW also) observed the teaching approach used in PLTW engineering courses. She noted that the methods of having students work on projects and learn to be learners "made sense to her" as a means to address the gap in basic science knowledge that some students brought with them to the school. In 2007, she decided to begin modifying the school's science curriculum to use a similar instructional approach as PLTW. As chair of the science department, she also revamped the freshman science curriculum and added a new course, Foundations of Science. The new course was specifically designed to help the students who were not enrolled in PLTW's Biomedical Science program. The new course used a similar instructional method to help strengthen their core skills and prepare them to successfully participate in 10th grade biology. For example, the course taught the skill of writing lab reports using the same format that was used in upper-level science courses such as chemistry and physics.

STRATEGY 3 • ENGAGE MATH, SCIENCE, AND PLTW TEACHERS IN COLLABORATIVE PLANNING & INSTRUCTION

To connect students' learning experiences across PLTW, math, and science curriculums, instructors purposefully collaborate to integrate their curriculums and instruction. Meaningful integration occurs when the instructors work side by side to map out curriculums, identify where content overlaps between their courses, and plan lessons and projects that connect and reinforce content across disciplines.

Still, the extent to which instructors practice cross-curricular integration varies considerably. A primary reason for this variation is that instructors often lack scheduled time to work together on curriculum analysis and instructional planning. Although some instructors may take the initiative to reach out to colleagues on their own, there is little evidence that the cross-content collaboration and integration that is at the foundation of a STEM culture can occur without a formalized process to drive it. To establish this, school leaders provide instructors with the time to plan collaboratively, and they set guidelines and expectations for what integration should look like in practice. Ideally, this occurs through weekly common planning time, but most important is that the expectation for collaboration is set and the time for collaboration is provided.

As noted in the section on project-based instruction, we suspect that many teachers are unlikely to link content from their STEM specialty course into a related math or science course unless the expectation to do so is clearly articulated by school leadership. Furthermore, that expectation has to be supported by time and any needed professional development.

As indicated previously, the leadership team assumes a critical role in providing the opportunity for teachers to plan collaboratively.

The Strategy in Action

EDISON MIDDLE SCHOOL

According to Edison's principal, the organization of students and teachers makes the middle school model "tailor made to do integration." At Edison, students were organized into two cohorts per grade and students took each of their core content courses with their cohort. English and social studies teachers worked together on one team and math and science teachers partnered on another team.

Then the four seventh-grade math/science teachers who were responsible for integrating PLTW into the math/science curriculum met at least once a week for approximately one hour.

The school leadership set the expectation that teachers were to engage in collaborative planning and "rich conversation" during these meetings. This expectation helped drive the strong collaboration that occurred among the seventh grade math/science team members. Although this middle school teacher team was committed to its instructional approach, the leadership team ensured that its collaboration was formal and had a platform to sustain it over time and through potential staffing changes.

During their meetings, the teachers addressed their instructional plans, developed shared materials, and divided up various responsibilities. They established team norms, defined the purpose of their team, and also developed an agenda to guide the direction of each meeting. These teachers emphasized that the "team concept is phenomenal."

Working as a cohesive unit, the teacher team members taught similar lessons, assigned the same projects, and used common assessments. They said that by working together as a team, they "think outside of the box and bounce ideas off of each other."

CLEARBROOK-GONVICK SCHOOL

At CGS, there were two teachers trained in delivery of Principles of Engineering (POE). One POE teacher was also a math teacher and one was also a science teacher. These two teachers collaborated to modify the delivery of the POE course so that it maximized their respective areas of expertise as teachers.

Many students found the math content of POE very challenging at the ninth grade level. To address this concern, in the 2012–2013 school year, CGS planned to create two classes of POE and then share instructional responsibilities between the two instructors. The idea was to organize the math-intensive and science-intensive content of POE to match the school's two semesters. During the first semester, one group of students would be taught by the POE/mathematics instructor to cover the more math-intensive content.

At the same time, another group of students would be taught by the POE/science instructor who would cover the more science-intensive content.

At the beginning of the second semester, the groups of students were to be switched so that each group would receive the more math-intensive or more science-intensive content with the other POE instructor. Some POE content may be particularly sequential in nature and therefore would be taught at critical junctures in the course, regardless of the relative expertise of the instructor. But, where feasible, this departmentalization of math-intensive content and science-intensive content allowed for extra support the students needed.

THOMAS WORTHINGTON HIGH SCHOOL

At TWHS, efforts to establish a strong and collaborative STEM focus for the school met with some initial challenges. Although many individual teachers embraced the possibility of collaboration, departmental administrators had concerns about the impact that cross-curricular collaboration and integration might have on scheduling and other responsibilities. In 2008–2009, PTLW teachers met extensively with departmental administrators and ultimately gained their acceptance for the formation of a STEM Collaborative Team. The STEM Collaborative Team was designed to help formalize and bring consistency to the process of teacher-to-teacher collaboration and planning. According to one PLTW teacher, "We always had a good relationship with the science staff, but once we showed them how the PLTW curriculum related, the collaboration really took off." This may have been aided, in part, by the fact that one of the physics teachers was a former engineer, so he had an affinity to the PLTW program.

Approximately 12 teachers served on the STEM Collaborative Team. Building leaders selected the team members based on who they felt would be forward thinking, flexible, and invested. The school's leadership team ensured that a planning team would focus on math, science and technology at each grade level. Members of the STEM Collaborative Team met weekly, and the building administrators scheduled common planning periods to facilitate teacher interaction and coordination.

Teachers at TWHS seemed to appreciate the ability to build connections between PLTW and STEM. A geometry teacher explained, "For us, STEM means problem-based learning. I was a hands-on learner, so I connect with students like that. Any way we can get students to have that 'aha' moment is important." Another math teacher added, "Teaching STEM math has taken lots of extra work to develop the lessons. But the payoff is great. For me, collaboration has been the best. Working with other teachers makes me a better teacher."

With approval from the school leadership, the PLTW teachers and other teachers on the STEM Collaborative Team set aside a planning period during which they could observe their fellow teachers in action. This allowed them to deeply absorb the content from these related courses, facilitating a deeper level of integration and collaboration.

THE STEM SCHOOLS CONTINUUM

In this chapter, we have explored three overarching components of building a STEM School:

1. *Laying a foundation of school-improvement strategies;*
2. *Providing a thorough implementation of a specialty STEM program (or programs); and,*
3. *Implementing strategies to develop a STEM culture.*

Within the last component relating to STEM culture, we identified three strategies:

1. *Establish Shared Guiding Principles for STEM Learning*
2. *Implement Innovative STEM Curriculum and Instruction*
3. *Engage Math, Science, and PLTW Teachers in Collaborative Planning and Instruction*

As we conducted the research phase of the project, we discovered a wide variety of approaches in how the schools and districts we studied approached STEM education. To make sense of this variety of approaches, we realized we were not observing a single, one-size-fits-all way of doing "STEM." In fact, none of the nine sites we observed were acting on every one of the strategies we identified.

Instead of one approach, we discovered a "STEM Schools Continuum" along which schools fall.

On one end of the continuum are schools in which specialty STEM courses provide an excellent learning experience to students, but the courses stand apart and do not connect to other courses that fall under the STEM umbrella.

In schools along the middle of the continuum were schools in which teachers—on a case-by-case basis and through individual initiative—inculcate some of the project-based and inquiry-based approaches of the specialty STEM courses into the math and science courses that they teach. They may informally collaborate with colleagues in other content areas to create a smattering of integrated or linked curriculum units.

Further along the continuum were schools that actively and intentionally create integrated and connected learning between STEM courses, and in some cases with other courses such as English language arts and the social sciences. In these schools, teachers actively and consistently collaborated with the support of administrative team members.

But even in those schools that were doing the most with building a STEM culture, leaders were emphatic that there was more work to be done. Their journey along the continuum continues.

What is important about this STEM Schools Continuum is that it doesn't matter so much where you currently sit on the curriculum, but rather what your plans are to develop a vision and move forward toward that vision.

REFLECTION QUESTIONS

Where does our school or district fall along the STEM Schools Continuum?

What aspects of "Building a strong school-improvement infrastructure" is solid with my school? Which aspects are weak or missing?

What other aspects of school-improvement have we implemented?

What aspects of "Implementing a specialty STEM program" is solid in my school? Which aspects are strong or missing?

Thoroughly plan the STEM program implementation.

- *Select and support a strong instructional team.*
- *Plan to reach all (or most) students.*
- *Reach out to local businesses to gain and sustain support.*
- *Reach out to prospective students.*
- *What aspects of "Taking action to develop a school-wide STEM culture" is solid in my school? Which aspects are weak or missing?*

Establish shared guiding principles for STEM learning.

- *Define STEM literacy*
- *Define STEM education*
- *Develop District-wide vision for STEM learning*

Implement innovative STEM curriculum and instruction

- *Integrate STEM-rich instruction across math, science, and other specialty STEM programs.*
- *Implement inquiry-based & project-based learning strategies*
- *Engage math, science and specialty-STEM teachers in collaborative planning and instruction*

In the next chapter, we lay out the action steps you can consider. These action steps are targeted relative to your role and responsibilities—whether you are a site-based school leader, a district STEM coordinator or administrator, or someone with a regional or national policy or philanthropic perspective.

CHAPTER 4

ACTION STEPS FOR CREATING A STEM SCHOOL

As we explore the STEM Schools Continuum, it is exciting to consider how a school can move from offering a single specialty STEM program that engages a few students (often the ones who were already interested and excited about STEM subjects) to adopting the policies and practices that could provide all students with focused, sustained, and purposeful STEM-rich learning experiences.

A specialty STEM program like PLTW can serve as an excellent starting point for a greater focus on STEM-related learning, but it is not realistic to hope that implementing just one or two specialty STEM programs will transform teaching and learning throughout a school. Nor will the programs, by themselves, create a culture shift toward the integration of STEM knowledge and skills for the large majority of students.

THE CALL FOR STEM LEADERSHIP

School leaders have a critical role to play in fostering STEM education, both in leading and in setting expectations, and creating a supportive environment for innovation and collaboration. A school simply cannot make the full shift from offering a STEM program to becoming a STEM school without a school leader who is leading.

In some of the schools we observed, teachers were highly entrepreneurial and drove the effort to develop cross-curricular connections. In these schools, the school leader provided encouragement and time for collaboration and also engaged other stakeholders in the school to buy into the STEM initiative.

In other schools, the school leader (or district-level leader) provided the impetus for the STEM initiative, helping set a vision for the effort and engaging staff members to take specific responsibilities for the effort.

In either case, for the STEM initiative to reach fruition, the school or district leader had to be actively involved and be a champion for the effort.

In this chapter, we lay out a series of strategies and action steps. The first set of strategies (1-5) is focused on the local leader at the school building. You cannot tackle all of these strategies at once, but they will give you the structure you need to get started and continue moving forward.

The next set of strategies (6-9) is applicable to not only local leaders, but also people who exert influence over the direction of STEM education as state education agency staff or state policymakers, federal agency staff or policymakers, or leaders in philanthropy.

SECTION 1
STRATEGIES & ACTION STEPS FOR LOCAL LEADERS

ESTABLISH SHARED GUIDING PRINCIPLES FOR STEM LEARNING

> ### *Action Steps*

Define STEM Education

Begin the process by reviewing the landscape of STEM education, both core STEM classes and specialty STEM programs, in your school to discover what assets you have to build upon.

Convene a working group of teachers and school administrators to study STEM education resources and create a working definition of STEM education for your school. Find out whether the state or your district has already created definitions or policies that you should consider.

Decide how your school will address the balance of "STEM-for-all" (STEM literacy) and opportunities for STEM expertise for especially motivated students.

Decide what kind of specialty STEM programs your school will offer, how they will be marketed to recruit a good gender and ethnic balance, and how you will deliver extra help for average-performing students participating in challenging STEM programs.

Define STEM Literacy

Create a definition of the knowledge, skills, and attributes that define STEM literacy in your school. Decide on the balance of broad, transferable problem solving and innovation skills, foundational concepts and principles, and career-specific technical skills.

Engage local employers to discover what STEM skills are used in their workplaces and how these employers can contribute real-world experiences to your STEM programs. Pay particular attention to workplaces that may heavily depend on technology and design but are not considered traditional STEM professions. Distinguish between careers that require STEM-literacy and careers that require STEM-expertise.

Decide how you will build student understanding about STEM careers and the educational paths required to access various careers. Don't assume that all good STEM careers require a four-year degree; many do not.

Decide how you will communicate the expectation of STEM literacy-for-all to the teaching faculty, the student body, and parents.

Decide how you will validate and document that students are developing STEM literacy. Find methods other than just standardized math and science assessments. Develop projects, activities, and simulations that will require students to demonstrate their STEM literacy.

Document all your decisions about STEM education and STEM literacy in a user-friendly written plan, and communicate the plan extensively to teachers, students, parents, and community partners.

Develop District-Wide Vision for STEM Learning

Adapt the school-based activities for defining STEM education and STEM literacy in ways that are appropriate for district-level leadership.

IMPLEMENT INNOVATIVE STEM CURRICULUM & INSTRUCTION

❯ Action Steps

Implement high-quality specialty STEM programs

Thoroughly plan the specialty STEM programs you want to launch by forming an advisory committee that can help gather information and provide ongoing input for the program.

Select and support a strong instructional team for each specialty STEM program, looking for teachers who possess a passion for instructional excellence and continuous professional growth and who thrive on collaborating with their peers. Make sure these instructors want to learn about and embrace project-based learning and other forms of active learning.

Plan to reach a substantial number of students by envisioning your specialty STEM programs as an integral component of the school's program offerings and as a component that will benefit most, if not all, students. Over time, the specialty STEM programs should be fully ingrained in the culture of the school.

Reach out and engage local employers and businesses so students have opportunities to interact often with professionals and observe and participate in real-world projects.

Reach out to prospective students to develop a pipeline of students enrolling in the specialty STEM program. Share information about the specialty STEM program with middle school students, and also consider hosting activities like summertime STEM camps and hands-on workshops at the high school for elementary and middle school children.

Integrate STEM-rich instruction across math, science, and other specialty STEM programs.

Ensure that each of your component STEM courses (e.g., math, science, engineering, computer technology, biotechnology) is built upon clear standards with a well-crafted curriculum. Each program must exhibit quality on its own before you try to develop an iSTEM (integrated STEM) approach.

To launch your iSTEM work, convene teachers to conduct detailed cross-walks of the standards and expectations within their respective courses.

As your math and science teachers implement new Common Core and Next Generation Science Standards, invite members of a cross-disciplinary team to become familiar with the new standards, so that integration and coordination will be easier to accomplish.

Encourage and support teachers to discuss their respective curricula and also to conduct multiple observations of one another's teaching. This will build a deeper understanding of the curriculum and will lay the groundwork for more effective collaboration.

Develop a small number of connected learning units and activities. Test the activities, fine tune them individually, and refine the collaborative planning process. Repeat the process, expanding your portfolio of learning units and activities.

Establish goals for the number of iSTEM activities you want to offer in each of your STEM courses. Also consider how to link STEM concepts into your English, social science, and arts programs.

Implement project-based and inquiry-based learning strategies.

Provide professional development for teachers to strengthen their skills in reworking their curriculum and instruction to use inquiry- and project-based learning approaches.

Provide ongoing peer coaching and school-based professional development.

Establish goals for teachers to use inquiry- and project-based learning, and integrate these expectations into teacher observation and evaluation processes.

Measure the impact on student learning and fine tune teacher practice through a continuous improvement process.

ENGAGE STEM TEACHERS IN COLLABORATIVE PLANNING & INSTRUCTION

➤ *Action Steps*

Create an "Innovation Team" to develop and pilot test the collaborative planning process for iSTEM.

Support collaborative planning times, either through common planning time built into the school day, through regular after-school meetings, or through concentrated planning activities during summer breaks.

As the Innovation Team conducts its work, have members share with the rest of the faculty the progress the team is making.

Create plans to open up the iSTEM process to other teachers so that the original Innovation Team does not engender suspicion or charges of favoritism.

SHARPEN THE FOCUS ON TECHNOLOGY & ENGINEERING

In past discussions about STEM, the term STEM becomes a proxy for science and mathematics, with technology and engineering as an afterthought. Math and science are required components of the core curriculum; technology and engineering are typically seen as nice-to-have electives but not essential to preparing America's youth for future success.

But math and science courses of the past do not pay sufficient attention to what the National Science Board identifies as "spatial talent."

> *Spatially talented students may not fit the classic model of what parents, the public, and even educators think of as "gifted." Rather than excelling in a typical classroom, these individuals might actively engage in vocational or career training classes or in projects outside of school where they can perform hands-on activities in three dimensions. These students may gravitate to engineering classes if offered early in the curriculum. Individuals with spatial abilities are routinely overlooked because these abilities are rarely measured and, if they are, the results often are not given the proper attention. This is an untapped pool of talent critical for our highly technological society.*[53]

Engineering and technology are critical components of STEM because they draw on and develop the spatial talents of students. Further, engineering and technology allow many students to see the real connections between education and the innovation economy in which they will soon live and work.

K-12 TECHNOLOGY EDUCATION

According to the National Academies, "Technology education today is the study of the human-made world, including artifacts, processes, and their underlying principles and concepts, and the overarching goal of technology education is to equip students to participate effectively in our technologically dependent world."[54]

In short, technology education entails an understanding of the use, purposes and benefits of technology. Unfortunately, when most people hear the term "technology" used in the content of STEM, they invariably think about students knowing how to use "computer technology" or "information technology," the most familiar uses of the term technology.

The International Association of Technical and Engineering Educators has defined the technology-related competencies that students need in five areas: 1) the nature of technology, 2) technology and society, 3) design, 4) abilities for a technological world" and 5) the designed world.

As a separate discipline, only a handful of states require students to participate in a technology course at some point during their K-12 education experience. A recent survey indicated that just seven states maintain some sort of technology education requirement, down from 12 states that reported this requirement in 2007.[55]

A 2004 report on technology education indicated there were approximately 35,909 technology education teachers, slightly fewer than had been reported in 2001.[56] This compares to approximately 276,000 middle and high school mathematics teachers, and 247,000 science teachers.[57]

K-12 ENGINEERING EDUCATION

K-12 engineering education is even more rare than technology education, although many technology education, math and science teachers have been cross-trained to teach engineering. There are an estimated 18,000 teachers who have received pre-service or in-service training for engineering education.

The National Academy of Engineering (NAE) estimates, out of nearly 56 million public and private K-12 students in the U.S., no more than 6 million young people have had any kind of formal engineering education.[58] [59]

The National Science Board, which focused its work specifically on filling the pipeline of STEM-intensive careers (vs. a STEM-literacy-for-all focus), emphasizes the importance of focusing on engineering. It said, "Engineering is a field critical to innovation, and exposure to engineering activities (e.g., robotics and invention competitions) can spark further interest in STEM. However, exposure to engineering at the pre collegiate level is exceedingly rare."[60]

NEW SCIENCE FRAMEWORK & NEXT GENERATION SCIENCE STANDARDS

This disparity and disconnect between mandatory science education and elective courses in engineering and technology has not been overlooked by organizations thinking about improvements needed for science education. In 2009, the National Academies convened a panel to develop a new "Framework for K-12 Science Education" around which the Next Generation Science Standards were developed. The Framework recommends a strong emphasis for engineering and technology education. "Engineering and technology are featured alongside the natural sciences (physical science, life sciences, and earth and space sciences) for two critical reasons: (1) to reflect the importance of understanding the human-built world and (2) to recognize the value of better integrating the teaching and learning of science, engineering, and technology."[61]

The framework panel recognize the potential of integrating science, engineering and technology to inspire and attract more young people into STEM careers, and better prepare all students for a productive future. "Although not all students will choose to pursue careers in science, engineering, or technology, we hope that a science education based on the framework will motivate and inspire a greater number of people –and a better representation of the broad diversity of the American population—to follow these paths than is the case today."[62]

The Next Generation Science Standards were built upon the framework, and thus, place a new emphasis on engineering and technology. "Science and engineering are integrated into science education by raising engineering design to the same level as scientific inquiry in science classroom instruction at all levels, and by emphasizing the core ideas of engineering design and technology applications."[63]

IMPLICATIONS FOR STEM LITERACY AND STEM EXPERTISE

The Next Generation Science Standards, with their enhanced focus on engineering and technology, and the new Common Core mathematics standards, have the potential to transform math and science courses into conduits for developing a foundation of STEM literacy for all students.

These positive reforms do not obviate the value of stand-alone engineering and technology programs, however. The standards themselves can be delivered through a variety of courses and environments, which can include engineering and technology courses.

Further, engineering and technology programs can help students go deeper into the application of science, particularly for students who are suited to pursue STEM-intensive careers.

➤ *Action Steps*

Carefully review the Next Generation Science Standards, and update and implement your science standards accordingly.

Provide sustained attention to the engineering and technology elements of the standards, so that during implementation, the science curriculum and instruction does not revert back to the more familiar approach, which is very light on engineering and technology elements.

SET OPERATIONAL GOALS FOR STEM LITERACY FOR ALL & STEM EXPERTISE FOR MANY

The philosophy of developing STEM culture neither assumes nor requires that every student aspire toward an engineering or science career. Rather, it recognizes that the tenets of STEM literacy—such as problem solving, creative thinking, and analytical thinking—are skills and habits of the mind in which all citizens should be proficient, and that a smaller percentage of citizenry should become STEM experts.

➤ *Action Steps*

Define, communicate, and implement a vision of what constitutes a STEM-focused approach to learning and instruction and what skills and knowledge make a student STEM literate.

Develop and implement policies and practices geared specifically to helping the school continuously fulfill this vision and the creation of a STEM-for-all culture.

Provide a STEM-intensive experience for those students who are most interested and capable of developing a deep STEM capacity.

SECTION 2
ACTION STEPS FOR NATIONAL, STATE, AND LOCAL LEADERS

MAKE MATH AND SCIENCE COURSES MORE ENGAGING

Both the new Common Core math standards and the Next Generation Science Standards anticipate the extensive use of real-world applications. Students ask very honest questions when they say, "Am I ever going to use this in my life?" The honest answer probably is, "Whether or not you will use this depends on what career you pursue." But too many math and science teachers are not able to answer the ancillary question, "How does ANYONE use this in their work?"

Many math and science teachers simply love the content they teach for its inherent beauty and structure. But that is too big a stretch for the average student who struggles to grasp the concepts and content of the curriculum. Mathematics and science teachers should be able to cite specific examples of how the content they teach is used in real career applications.

Because many math and science teachers do not have the training or resources to answer these questions, it is unlikely they will readily offer the real-world applications called for by the new standards unless resources are developed and provided to them. Without these answers, many students will continue to struggle and may not put forth the effort needed to master the math and science standards.

➤ *Action Steps*

Create and share access to crosswalks between the Common Core math standards, the new Next Generation Science Standards, and specialty STEM programs like Project Lead The Way. These crosswalks can serve as the foundation for a curriculum resource project, in which a number of cross-curricular lessons/activities could be developed to be offered in math and science programs.

Design and share lessons to show the application and relevance of math and science content to specific STEM careers.

Sponsors of specialty STEM programs should create a searchable database of connected lessons and activities that are also linked to the cross-walk of standards and practices. These resources would demonstrate how core math or science teachers and teachers of specially STEM programs can offer coordinated and linked learning activities.

STRENGTHEN THE FOCUS ON STEM INNOVATION IN TYPICAL PUBLIC AND MIDDLE SCHOOLS

As noted earlier, one of the goals articulated in the report on STEM education by the President's Council of Advisors on Science and Technology is "Creating new STEM-focused schools." The National Science Board also recommended starting 1,000 STEM specialty schools over a 10-year period. According to estimates, there are currently about 100 STEM specialty schools in the United States.

STEM specialty schools provide an exciting and valuable part of the answer to enhancing America's educational competitiveness because they help cultivate STEM interest and skills and they test effective curriculum and approaches to teaching, learning, and connecting to real-world, community-based experiences. [64]

But realistically, these STEM specialty schools are not large enough and do not touch enough students to be the total answer for the nation's STEM challenge. All students need to be STEM literate, and students with greater talents and interests need to be cultivated to embrace rigorous and challenging STEM fields of studies.

Through our work on the *STEM Schools Project*, we have documented how the typical public high school and middle school, as well as private schools, can begin taking practical steps toward building a STEM culture for their students. The approaches we have identified will help public and private schools embed STEM culture and practices school-wide.

➤ *Action Steps*

National and state organizations should focus on typical public schools as the scalable solution to ensure large numbers of America's youths have STEM-related skills and thus strengthen American competitiveness.

DEVELOP PROFESSIONAL DEVELOPMENT TOOLS

The National Science Board notes that there is a growing body of research in recent decades that illuminates how children learn about science, technology, engineering and technology. This emerging research is making it possible to devise more effective instructional materials and teaching strategies.[65]

The Board also suggests that "in the STEM areas, all students, including the most talented, should have the opportunity to experience inquiry-based learning, peer collaboration, open-ended, real-world problem solving, hands-on training, and interactions with practicing scientists, engineers and other experts."[66]

Our observations during site visits indicate that although teachers are able to deliver a structured curriculum that utilizes project-based learning techniques, this does not mean the same teachers are necessarily able to adapt their current math and/or science curriculum into a project-based or inquiry-based format.

Teachers typically need initial professional development and support on the concepts of project-based learning, and guided practice in developing project-based lessons that target the same outcomes as more traditional existing curriculum. After initial professional development, they need ongoing peer support interactions, supplemented by periodic expert observation and feedback. Because most teachers cannot "drop everything and write new curriculum," they need to gradually develop resources, try them in the classroom, refine them, and build them into the routine of the curriculum.

➤ *Action Steps*

School leaders should secure professional development and ongoing support to develop project-based applications within their curriculum. [67]

Policymakers should make research about and funding for project-based learning professional development a priority.

SHARE PROMISING PRACTICES & RESEARCH FINDINGS THROUGH NATIONAL NETWORKS OF STEM SCHOOL LEADERS

One of the key findings from the case studies in the *STEM Schools Project* is the central role of the school leader in leading and supporting the movement toward a STEM school. A school simply cannot make the full movement from having a STEM program to becoming a STEM school unless the school leader is leading.

We suggest a concerted effort to share the findings from the *STEM Schools Project* and numerous other research findings about STEM education in a way that is targeted to school principals in the United States.

A sustained effort to identify promising schools and foster dialogue and learning among principals (as well as assistant principals, curriculum coordinators, and STEM coordinators) could make a very positive impact on the national STEM dialogue.

➤ *Action Steps*

Convene school leaders through a series of state-based events, national meetings, and virtual meetings to learn about promising practices and research findings.

Organize leaders into professional learning communities—small working groups where relationships among leaders can be developed—to share successes and challenges and provide peer coaching and encouragement; such learning communities will allow school leaders to more effectively put their knowledge into practice.

REFLECTION QUESTIONS

While it is still fresh, write down some notes related to each of the strategies discussed in this chapter.

What does my school or district need to do next for each of the following strategies?

- *Establish shared guiding principles for STEM learning*
- *Implement innovative STEM curriculum and instruction*
- *Engage STEM teachers in collaborative planning and instruction*
- *Sharpen the focus on technology and engineering*
- *Set operations goals for STEM literacy for all and STEM expertise for many*
- *Make math and science courses more engaging*
- *Strengthen the focus on STEM innovation in typical public and middle schools.*
- *Develop professional development tools for active learning strategies*
- *Share promising practices and research findings through national networks of STEM school leaders*

CONCLUSION

We have covered a lot of ground in the relatively few pages of this book. First we looked at the STEM challenge that is driving national, state, and local interest in STEM education. We learned about the *STEM Schools Project*, its guiding questions, and the nine sites that we studied during the project.

We noted that a strong school improvement structure, grounded in research-based practices, provides the foundation upon which to implement a high-quality STEM program and to launch a larger effort to build a STEM culture.

Furthermore, a strong specialty STEM program like Project Lead The Way is an excellent asset and is a great starting point for developing a STEM culture.

Finally, we observed that to develop a STEM culture, the leadership and instructional teams will need to find a shared understanding of what defines STEM education, what skill sets make a student STEM literate, and what the value is of thorough STEM- learning experiences to students and the larger community. Then they need to operationalize these understandings through designing curriculum, connecting and correlating curriculum, and adopting active-learning strategies. The operational changes only happen through extensive teacher collaboration and professional growth.

Beyond all these discussions of strategies and processes, our focus comes back to the several hundred young people who walk through your school doors and hallways each day.

They are facing a future of rapid technological change, incredible scientific advances, and a culture and society that demands more sophisticated analysis, decision making, and adaptability than, perhaps, ever before.

Will they be ready?

The end goal of our efforts is to cultivate young men and women who are skilled, ambitious and ready to face the STEM challenge of the 21st century.

To be ready, you want all your students to develop a real-world literacy—a STEM literacy. They will grasp core knowledge of science and math and be able to apply math and science concepts to real-world challenges. They will be able to utilize these STEM skills and extend them through a reasonable level of written and oral communication, teamwork, problem solving, and innovation.

You also want to develop a substantial number of students who are prepared to pursue education and careers that demand STEM expertise. These young people will go deeper in study of STEM disciplines in high school and will also set career goals in fields that require STEM expertise. Their paths will include exploration of and application and admission to postsecondary education programs in one of the STEM disciplines.

At some point in two to six years after successful completion of high school, almost all of your former students will enter the workforce. If your efforts at developing a STEM culture are successful, each year you will launch several hundred young men and women who are ready to take on the challenges of the 21st century economy.

If your colleagues -- leaders of America's 24,000 public middle and high school-- pursue the same agenda as you, one that engages teachers, students, families, and community partners, the United States could see an amazing renaissance in the quality of its workforce, in our economic fortunes, and in the health of our families and communities.

LEADERSHIP: A FINAL REFRAIN

This is the exciting opportunity, and it is the daunting responsibility of school leadership. You, the school leader, are leaving a legacy. Your legacy is not simply the academic scores or graduation rates upon which your school is measured in the short term; your real legacy is the young men and women who travel through your school for a time, learn and grow toward becoming responsible adults, and then enter the larger community to add to the health of our families, our communities, and our economic life.

Thank you. Remember, you are not alone but are joined by thousands of women and men in the same pursuit.

Godspeed.

ACKNOWLEDGMENTS

This work would not be complete without acknowledging the many individuals who helped bring it to life.

Michelle Hebert-Giffen from Meeder Consulting managed the overall effort of coordinating research, developing the case studies and provided valuable editing of the final report. Jennifer Grams, Nichole Jackson, and Leah Felcher helped conduct site visits and took the lead in writing our findings up into case studies. Kelly Livieratos of Patapsco Editorial Services provided editorial support for each of the case studies.

Karen Wilken of the Kern Family Foundation provided insight into the initial development of the STEM Schools Project, and Ryan Olson of the Foundation offered valuable advice and guidance in crafting the final report. The Kern Family Foundation provided generous financial support to the research phase and writing of the project case studies.

The findings in this book are derived from the on-the-ground work carried out by creative and dedicated educators at all of the case study sites. We cannot list the name of every educator with whom we met, but we would like to acknowledge those who took a lead in coordinating the site visits and providing additional clarifications during our research process. These are:

Clearbrook-Gonvick School: District superintendent Allen Ralston and high school principal Kristil McDonald.

Edison Middle School: Janesville School District Career and Technical Education Coordinator Steve Huth and Principal Jim Lemire.

Greenfield-Central High School: School Principal Steve Bryant.

Lenawee Intermediate School District: District superintendent Jim Philps and STEM Services Director Kim Salsbury.

Pine River-Backus School: Superintendent Cathy Bettino, Principal Trent Langemo, and school counselor Ms. Mary Ruth Sigan.

Saint Thomas More High School: Principal Dr. Mark Joerres and Curriculum Coordinator Mary Burke.

Wheeling High School: Principal Dr. Lazaro Lopez.

Thomas Worthington High School: Principal James Gaskill and STEM Academy teacher Bryan Brown.

Numerous other individuals from within the Project Lead The Way network and with responsibilities for STEM education inside state education agencies provided input to the research phase of the *STEM Schools Project.*

To all these individuals, named and unnamed, who generously shared ideas, advice, and experiences, and to those teachers who opened up their classrooms for us to see their work and that of their students, thank you!

APPENDIX 1

PROJECT LEAD THE WAY (PLTW) PROGRAMS & COURSE TITLES

PLTW offers two programs at the high school level: Pathway to Engineering and Biomedical Sciences. The Gateway to Technology Program is offered in middle schools.

PATHWAY TO ENGINEERING (PTE)

The PLTW Pathway To Engineering (PTE) program is designed to provide students with experience in the engineering design process.

- *Foundation Courses*
  Introduction to Engineering Design (IED)
  Principles of Engineering (POE)

- *Specialization Courses*
  Aerospace Engineering (AE)
  Biotechnical Engineering (BE)
  Civil Engineering and Architecture (CEA)
  Computer Integrated Manufacturing (CIM)
  Digital Electronics (DE)

- *Capstone Course*
  Engineering Design and Development (EDD)

BIOMEDICAL SCIENCES (BMS)

Designed to prepare students for post-secondary study or future careers in the biomedical sciences field, the PLTW Biomedical Sciences (BMS) Program focuses on human medicine and related topics such as physiology, genetics, microbiology and public health.

- ***Foundation Courses***
  Principles of the Biomedical Sciences (PBS)
  Human Body Systems (HBS)
  Medical Interventions (MI)

- ***Capstone Course***
  Biomedical Innovation (BI)

GATEWAY TO TECHNOLOGY (GTT)

Implemented in grades six through eight, the PLTW Gateway to Technology (GTT) program is designed to foster students' interest in STEM learning.

- ***Foundation Units***
  Automation and Robotics (AR)
  Design and Modeling (DM)

- ***Specialization Units***
  Energy and the Environment (EE)
  Flight and Space (FS)
  Green Architecture (GA)
  Magic of Electrons (ME)
  Science of Technology (ST)

APPENDIX 2

SAMPLING OF CLASSROOM-BASED & EXTRA-CURRICULAR STEM PROGRAMS

Academy of Engineering, National Academy Foundation • naf.org

Academy of Information Technology, National Academy Foundation • naf.org

National Math & Science Initiative Advanced Placement Program, National Math & Science Initiative • www.nationalmathandscience.org/programs/ap-training-incentive-programs

Battlebots IO, National Trade and Manufacturers Association www.botsiq.org/manage.aboutbbiq.php

BEST Robotics, Affiliation with Auburn University • best.eng.auburn.edu

Engineering is Elementary, Boston Museum of Science www.mos.org/eie/index.php

Engineering the Future, Boston Museum of Science www.mos.org/etf/index.html

FIRST Robotics, FIRST • www.usfirst.org/roboticsprograms/frc

Ford Partnership for Advanced Studies (Ford PAS) Next Generation Learning, Ford Motor Company Fund • fordpas.org/

Full Option Science System (FOSS), Lawrence Hall of Science, University of California Berkeley • www.fossweb.com

Girlstart • www.girlstart.org

IMSA Fusion, Illinois Mathematics and Science Academy (IMSA) www3.imsa.edu/programs/fusion

Infinity Project, Caruth Institute for Engineering Education Southern Methodist University • www.smu.edu/Lyle/Infinity

Intel Math Program, University of Arizona • math.arizona.edu/~ime/intelmath

Maker Faire, MAKE Magazine • makerfaire.com

Merck Institute for Science Education (MISE), The Merck Company Foundation www.mise.org/secure/index.html

MIT Science and Engineering Program for Teachers, Massachusetts Institute of Technology • web.mit.edu/scienceprogram/index.html

Real World Design Challenge • www.realworlddesignchallenge.org

Sally Ride Science • www.sallyridescience.com

Science Career Ladder, The New York Hall of Science • www.nysci.org/learn/scl

Science Technology Concepts Program, Smithsonian Institution National Science Resources Center • www.nsrconline.org/index.html

Seeds of Science/Roots of Reading Curriculum, The Lawrence Hall of Science, UC Berkley and UC Berkley Graduate School of Education www.scienceandliteracy.org

Starbase 2.0, Department of Defense – Wright Patterson Air Force Base edoutreach.wpafb.af.mil/starbase/index.html

ST Math, MIND Research Institute • www.mindresearch.net/index.php

STEMWORKS Database, Change the Equation • changetheequation.org/improving-philanthropy/stemworks

Team America Rocketry Challenge, Aerospace Industries Association (AIA) and the National Association of Rocketry (NAR) • www.rocketcontest.org

Techbridge, Chabot Space & Science Center • techbridgegirls.org/Home.aspx

UTeach, The University of Texas at Austin (UT Austin) • uteach-institute.org

Vex Robotics, Vex Robotics Inc. • www.vexrobotics.com

Web Based Inquiry Science Environment (WISE), UC Berkley • wise.berkeley.edu/webapp/index.html

REFERENCES
(Endnotes)

[1] National Academy of Engineering and National Research Council of the National Academies. (2009). Introduction. In *Engineering in K-12 Education: Understanding the Status in Improving the Prospects*. Washington, D.C.: National Academies Press, 2009.

[2] President's Council of Advisors on Science and Technology (PCAST). (2010). Prepare and Inspire: K–12 Science, Technology, Engineering, and Math (STEM) Education for America's Future. Working Group Report. Washington, DC: The White House. Retrieved from www.whitehouse.gov/sites/default/files/microsites/ostp/pcast-stemed-report.pdf.

[3] Retrieved from Maryland Board of Education, April 4, 2013. www.marylandpublicschools.org/MSDE/programs/stem

[4] In the workplace, individuals with different STEM specializations often collaborate on multidisciplinary teams to conduct basic research, apply basic research to developing innovations, and commercialize innovations into marketable goods and services. However, for the most part, education is delivered to students in isolated contact and is abstracted from the real-world contexts in which the subject matter was originally discovered or developed.

The concept of iSTEM is to draw connections between the silos of content to provide a more authentic and engaging learning experience. This iSTEM approach was demonstrated by several of the schools in the *STEM Schools Project*, the case study research carried out by Meeder Consulting.

Because it mimics real-world experience, it seems that the iSTEM approach would engage students more deeply and improve student learning. But as an educational methodology, iSTEM is still relatively untested.

To address this gap in knowledge, the National Academy of Engineering and the Board on Science Education has created a committee to conduct a study to develop a research agenda for determining the approaches and conditions most likely to lead to positive outcomes of iSTEM education at the K–12 level. The committee is working to characterize existing approaches to iSTEM education, including programs offered in after-school and informal settings, and is reviewing the evidence for the impact of integrated STEM on student awareness of and interest, motivation, and achievement in STEM subjects.

[5] National Academy of Engineering of the National Academies, Toward Integrated STEM Education: Developing A Research Agenda, www.nae.edu/Projects/iSTEM.aspx Retrieved April 5, 2013.

[6] Gonzales, P., Williams, T., Jocelyn, L., Roey, S., Kastberg, D., & Brenwald, S. (2009). Highlights from TIMSS 2007: Mathematics and Science Achievement of U.S. Fourth- and Eighth-Graders in an International Context. Washington, DC: U.S. Department of Education.

[7] National Science Board. (2010). Science and Engineering Indicators: 2010. Arlington, VA: National Science Foundation. Retrieved from www.nsf.gov/statistics/seind10/start.htm.

[8] Executive summary, Nation's Report Card, Mathematics 2011: Summary of Results, Retrieved from: nces.ed.gov/nationsreportcard.

[9] President's Council of Advisors on Science and Technology (PCAST). (2010).

[10] Lowell, B. L., Salzman, H., Bernstein, H., & Henderson, E. (2009). *Steady as She Goes: Three Generations of Students through the Science and Engineering Pipeline*. Paper presented at the Annual Meeting of the Association for Public Policy Analysis and Management, Washington, DC, November 5–7. Retrieved from policy.rutgers.edu/faculty/salzman/SteadyAsSheGoes.pdf.

[11] Hill, C., Corbett, C., & St. Rose, A. (2010). *Why So Few? Women in Science, Technology, Engineering, and Mathematics*. Washington, DC: AAUW. Retrieved from www.aauw.org/research/why-so-few.

[12] National Science Foundation. (2009). *Women, Minorities, and Persons with Disabilities in Science and Engineering: 2009*. Arlington, VA: National Science Foundation. Retrieved from www.nsf.gov/statistics/wmpd.

[13] Ellison, G., & Swanson, A. (2010). *The Gender Gap in Secondary School Mathematics at High Achievement Levels: Evidence from the American Mathematics Competitions. Journal of Economic Perspectives 24*(2), 109–128.

[14] National Science Board, 2010, *Science and Engineering Indicators; 2010*. Arlington, VA: National Science Foundation. Chapter 2. Accessible at www.nsf.gov/statistics/seind10/start.htm.

[15] President's Council of Advisors on Science and Technology (PCAST). (2010).

[16] National Science Foundation, Division of Science Resources Statistics, *Survey of Earned Doctorates*, Retrieved from www.nsf.gov/statistics/nsf09311/pdf/nsf09311.pdf

[17] National Science Board, 2010, *Science and Engineering Indicators; 2010*. Arlington, VA: National Science Foundation. Chapter 2. Retrieved from www.nsf.gov/statistics/seind10/c2/c2h.htm

[18] Solow, R. M. (1957). Technical Change and the Aggregate Production Function. *Review of Economics and Statistics 39*, 312–320, 1957.

[19] Helpman, Elhanan. (2004). *The Mystery of Economic Growth*. Cambridge, MA: Harvard University Press.

[20] Committee on Prospering in the Global Economy of the 21st Century: An Agenda for American Science and Technology, National Academy of Sciences, National Academy of Engineering, Institute of Medicine. (2005). Rising Above The Gathering Storm: Energizing and Employing America for a Brighter Economic Future. Washington, DC: National Academies Press. Retrieved from www.nap.edu/catalog.php?record_id=11463.

[21] President's Council of Advisors on Science and Technology (PCAST). (2010).

[22] U.S. Department of Commerce (2011), *STEM: Good Jobs Now and for the Future*, ESA Issue Brief #03-11, July 2011, Economics and Statistics Administration. Retrieved from www.esa.doc.gov/sites/default/files/reports/documents/stemfinalyjuly14_1.pdf.

[23] U.S. Census Bureau (2008), An Older and More Diverse Nation by Midcentury, News Release, August 14, 2008, Washington, DC. Retrieved from www.census.gov/newsroom/releases/archives/population/cb08-123.

[24] President's Council of Advisors on Science and Technology (PCAST). (2010).

[25] Ibid.

[26] Committee on Prospering in the Global Economy of the 21st Century: An Agenda for American Science and Technology, National Academy of Sciences, National Academy of Engineering, Institute of Medicine. (2005). Rising Above The Gathering Storm: Energizing and Employing America for a Brighter Economic Future. Washington, DC: National Academies Press. Retrieved from www.nap.edu/catalog.php?record_id=11463.

[27] See Common Core State Standards Initiative • www.corestandards.org.

[28] See Next Generation Science Standards • www.nextgenscience.org.

[29] President's Council of Advisors on Science and Technology (PCAST). (2010).

[30] Committee on Prospering in the Global Economy of the 21st Century: An Agenda for American Science and Technology, National Academy of Sciences, National Academy of Engineering, Institute of Medicine. (2005). Rising Above The Gathering Storm: Energizing and Employing America for a Brighter Economic Future. Washington, DC: National Academies Press. Retrieved from www.nap.edu/catalog.php?record_id=11463.

[31] Ibid.

[32] Ibid.

[33] National Science Board (2010). *Preparing the Next Generation of STEM Innovators: Identifying and Developing Our Nation's Human Capital.* Arlington, VA: National Science Foundation. Retrieved from www.nsf.gov/nsb/publications/2010/nsb1033.pdf.

[34] Ibid.

[35] Ibid.

[36] See the STEMx website at www.stemx.us.

[37] See the Change the Equation website at changetheequation.org.

[38] See the STEM Solutions website at usnewsstemsolutions.com/conference.

[39] National Science Board, 2010, Science and Engineering Indicators; 2010. Arlington, VA: National Science Foundation. Chapter 2. Accessible at www.nsf.gov/statistics/seind10/start.htm.

[40] White, S., & Tesfaye, C. L. (2010). High School Physics Courses and Enrollment. White Paper, August 2010. American Institute of Physics Statistical Research Center. Melville, NY: American Institute of Physics. Retrieved from www.aip.org/statistics/trends/reports/highschool3.pdf.

[41] Executive summary, Nation's Report Card, Mathematics 2011: Summary of Results, Retrieved from: nces.ed.gov/nationsreportcard.

[42] Ibid.

[43] Project Lead the Way, "Our History," retrieved March 7, 2013, from www.pltw.org/about-us/our-history.

[44] Tai, Robert H., "An Examination of the Research Literature on Project Lead the Way," November 2012, Retrieved from www.pltw.org/sites/default/files/PLTW%20DR.TAI%20-%20brochure_pages.pdf.

[45] Schenk Jr., T., et al (2011), "Achievement outcomes of Project Lead The Way: A study of the impact of PLTW in Iowa (working paper). Retrieved from: www.cesmee.iastate.edu/brownbags/PLTW_JEE%20paper%20Sep-29-11.pdf

[46] The National Academies Committee on Integrated STEM. Meeting information can be retrieved from www8.nationalacademies.org/cp/meetingview.aspx?MeetingID=6125&MeetingNo=4.

[47] Engineering is Elementary. See www.eie.org.

[48] LISD STEM Services Advisory Committee Handbook. (2012) Lenawee Intermediate School District, Adrian, Michigan.

49 Worthington STEM Literacy Pyramid, adapted from "STEM Literacy: Pathways to Education, Workforce, and Innovation," Leigh R. Abts, PhD, University of Maryland. Copy of presentation retrieved from www.orau. org/leadershipsummit/pdf/abts.pdf.

50 Cardinal Communities, "Thomas Worthington High School: Renewal Plan," May 27, 2011.

51 The Partnership for 21st Century Skills is a national organization that advocates for 21st century readiness for every student. The organizations advocates for core academic skills as well as the "4Cs (Critical thinking and problem solving, Communication, Collaboration, and Creativity and innovation)." Retrieved at: www.p21.org

52 Project-Based Learning online resource, retrieved October 24, 2012 from www.pbl-online.org/About/whatisPBL.htm.

53 National Science Board (2010). Preparing the Next Generation of STEM Innovators: Identifying and Developing Our Nation's Human Capital. Arlington, VA: National Science Foundation. Retrieved from www.nsf.gov/ nsb/publications/2010/nsb1033.pdf.

54 National Academy of Engineering and National Research Council of the National Academies. (2009).

55 Moye et al (2012), The Status of Technology and Engineering Education in the United States: A Fourth Report of the Findings From the States (2011-12), Technology and Engineering Teacher, May/June 2012. Retrieved from www.iteaconnect.org/TAA/LinkedFiles/Articles/TTTpdf/2011- 12Volume71/StatusofTEE.Moye.Dugger.Starkweather.2012.pdf.

56 The 2012 survey by Moye had too few respondents on this question to provide a reasonable estimate about the current number of technology education teachers. Moye et al (2012), The Status of Technology and Engineering Education in the United States: A Fourth Report of the Findings From the States (2011-12), Technology and Engineering Teacher, May/June 2012. Retrieved from www.iteaconnect.org/TAA/ LinkedFiles/Articles/TTTpdf/2011-12Volume71/StatusofTEE.Moye.Dugger. Starkweather.2012.pdf.

57 NCES (National Center for Education Statistics). 2009. Teacher Attrition and Mobility: Results From the 2004-05 Teacher Follow-up Survey. First Look. Table 2 and Table 3. U.S. Department of Education. Available online at: nces.ed.gov/pubs2007/2007307.pdf

58 National Academy of Engineering and National Research Council of the National Academies. (2009)

59 U.S. Department of Education (2008), National Center for Education Statistics. Digest of Education Statistics, 2007 (NCES 2008-022).

[60] National Science Board (2010). *Preparing the Next Generation of STEM Innovators: Identifying and Developing Our Nation's Human Capital.* Arlington, VA: National Science Foundation. Retrieved from www.nsf.gov/nsb/publications/2010/nsb1033.pdf.

[61] National Research Council. (2012). *A Framework for K-12 Science Education: Practices, Crosscutting Concepts, and Core Ideas.* Committee on a Conceptual Framework for New K-12 Science Education Standards. Board on Science Education, Division of Behavioral and Social Sciences and Education. Washington, DC: The National Academies Press.

[62] Ibid.

[63] Achieve, Inc. (2013), Next Generation Science Standards, Executive Summary, June 2013, Achieve, Inc, Washington, DC. Retrieved from www.nextgenscience.org/sites/ngss/files/Final%20Release%20NGSS%20Front%20Matter%20-%206.17.13%20Update_0.pdf

[64] For an example of a specialty STEM school, Manor New Tech High School, located in Manor, Texas, is a small STEM high school, affiliated with the New Tech High network, and makes extensive use of project-based and inquiry-based instruction. Learn more about Manor New Tech at manornewtech.com.

[65] See National Research Council. (2005). How Students Learn: History, Mathematics, and Science in the Classroom. Washington, DC: National Academies Press.) (20. National Research Council. (2007). Taking Science to School. Washington, DC: National Academies Press.)

[66] Notes from the National Science Board Preparing the Next Generation of STEM Innovators" suggest review of Olson, S. & Loucks-Horsley, S (Eds.). (2000). Inquiry and the national science education standards; a guide for teaching and learning. Committee on the Development of an Addendum to the National Science Education Standards of Scientific Inquiry, National Research Council. Washington, DC: National Academies Press.

[67] The Buck Institute for Education provides a wealth of information and resources about project-based learning. See www.bie.org.